God-gebra 101

Discovering...The Value of "X"

By Ivan Blacksmith

PublishAmerica
Baltimore

ISBN: 1-60441-636-X
PUBLISHED BY PUBLISHAMERICA, LLLP
www.publishamerica.com
Baltimore

Printed in the United States of America

Table of Contents

Acknowledgments

This book is dedicated to my beautiful wife Melanie (for your strength and encouragement) and my two wonderful children, Blair and Ivonna. To my lovely mother, you always believed in me. To my wonderful mother-in-law "Nursie": For your unwavering support. To Elder Ben and Sis. Shayla Jones: For imparting the vision. I am further indebted to The Mighty Men of Valor; J.C. (Rodney), Sean, Dolphus and Jeff. To my Spiritual parents; Pastor Joseph Hewitt and Lady Portia Hewitt and the Reconciliation Word Ministry ("US" Family). To the reader: If God says it, believe it and watch Him bring it to pass. God Bless You!

God-gebra 101

Discovering...The Value of "X"

Preface

In elementary algebra, letters are used to stand for numbers. For example, in the equation a+b+c=x, the letters *a, b,* and *c* stand for various known constant numbers called coefficients. The letter **x is an unknown variable** whose value depends on the values of *a, b,* and *c,* and may be determined by solving the equation. Much of classical algebra is concerned with finding solutions to equations or systems of equations (i.e., finding the value of the unknowns), that upon substitution into the original equation will make it a numerical identity.

The equation (a+b+c=x) is very present in our lives today as many people perpetually experience situations that seem to be **a** - an impossibility. Circumstances in life bombard us and present themselves without being accompanied by a glaring resolution which causes us to consider our situations to be in a state that can best be described as **b** - beyond hope. However, it is during these times of uncertainty and doubt that we must be reminded, that our God has given us a **c** - certain measure of faith (Rom. 12:3) and our ability to find the value of **x** - (The God Factor), depends on how effectively we exercise our measure of faith to receive the victory.

This book is being written as an encouragement and motivation to individuals who because of controllable or perhaps un-controllable factors in life, were left physically or emotionally scarred, and for years have harbored feelings of abandonment, low self esteem, and even discouragement. And if the truth be told, you may have even questioned God by asking, "If you love me, why has my life been so painful?" Or maybe you asked, "How can my life have a positive outcome when it's been so full of negative influences?" God-gebra is uniquely designed to answer these inquiries. It also gives confidence and assurance to each person "going through" trials and tribulations that have shaken every ounce of faith they have mustered to believe that God will move mightily on their behalf. Also, my intent is to impart through this manuscript "So Great Faith" (Luke 7:9) and inspire courage to those who are apprehensive to step out of the boat, fulfill God's commanded exploits and "Walk on Water."

Remember, if you are in a situation that seems like there is no way out, or you're believing God for what others have declared to be impossible, let God apply the God-gebra" principle which says: *"With men this is impossible; but with God ALL THINGS ARE POSSIBLE* (Matt.19:26).

—Ivan Ross Blacksmith

Chapter 1
What Is God-gebra?

Initially, I would imagine, many of you glanced at this book and noticed the title and perhaps thought, "What is God-gebra? I've heard of algebra but what does God have to do with Algebra?"

Let me explain the origins behind the God-gebra concept.

It all started one day during a conversation with our children's God-parents, Elder Benjamin and Sis. Shayla Jones. This story centers around the year 1996—a time when my wife and I were looking to purchase our first home. Needless to say, we had been working with an agent who had not locked into our vision and in essence, became a hindrance to our faith as we searched for our new home. What do I mean? Well, let me explain further. My wife and I would complete our due diligence and locate homes that we felt were viable prospects and in turn, give them to our agent to schedule appointments for further evaluation. Throughout this process, she would sarcastically say, "This is probably going to be your third or fourth home, as you cannot afford this neighborhood." After a while, we noticed that in order for us to operate with the faith necessary to receive the promises of God, we were going to have to respectfully relieve her of her duties.

Shortly after this experience, The Jones' visited and we explained to them how frustrated we were with our agent and the first-time home buying process. We told Elder Jones that every home we liked was too expensive (we were told), and every home we could afford already had a deal pending. Then Elder Jones replied with a statement that would forever change our lives and our perspective of our God would never be the same again. Elder Jones laughed in his own encouraging way and said, "Take the handcuffs off of God. He can do anything! Don't worry about how God is going to do it. Your job is simply to believe He Can Do It." Then he introduced me to a word that I have never forgotten since and will remember for the rest of my life. He finalized his thoughts by saying, "Its God-gebra, that's how God does it! The more your situation makes no sense, the more God will make sense out of your situation." The God-gebra concept was born.

So by definition, God-gebra is the process by which God breaks the rules of logic and reason as we know them, and proverbially places a doorknob on a wall to make a way out of no way. God-gebra represents that new job you received without meeting the minimum qualification requirements. God-gebra includes being handpicked by God when naysayer's doubt your ability and anointing. God-gebra is made evident by starting a storefront ministry with limited funding that has now become a deliverance center and spiritual safe-haven for thousands. God-gebra becomes visible when God takes the needle out of the arm of a drug addict and places a Bible under that same arm—fills him with His spirit and uses him to minister to millions. God-gebra occurs when a single mother is abandoned by her husband to raise children alone. The odds say, "No, you can't make it!" But God says, "Yes, you can!!!" God-gebra is revealed when a job is lost and miraculously all the bills are paid.

God-gebra is at work when a couple is reconciled back to God and decides to re-marry after being divorced for years. It is the last word after the doctors have said, "There is nothing else we can do." God-gebra proclaims, *"I shall live and not die and declare the works of the Lord"* (Psa.118:17). God-gebra, like its namesake Algebra, seeks to balance the equations of life, so that God's people come out on top and learn to believe on Him to fulfill all their needs according to His riches in glory.

God's Sovereignty

To lay the foundation of God-gebra, we have to first recognize and comprehend the awesome power of God. The scope of God's preeminence can best be described as sheer sovereignty. What is Sovereignty? The dictionary defines *sovereignty* as, *"one that exercises supreme, permanent authority."*

The word sovereign is traditionally used in correlation to kingship, because in former eras, many kings ruled with complete authority. They were not under the law, they *were* the law, and they exercised their influence in any manner they deemed appropriate.

If the truth be told, it takes revelation by the Holy Spirit to open our understanding to the vast knowledge and deep awareness of God's sovereignty. Because of our finite minds, many of us limit God. We put God in a box because we fail to comprehend the profoundness of His absolute control. The Bible begins with words that sum everything up: "In the beginning God…" (Gen. 1:1). Before there was an earth as we know it, God was. He is the Alpha and Omega; the first and the last. We are accustomed to limits, but He is limitless. We live in time, and He dwells in eternity. We sometimes face impossibilities, but nothing is impossible with God.

When God formed mankind from the dust of the ground, He breathed into him the breath of life and gave him something eternal, a living soul. Because of this breathtaking display of love and power, we are dependent upon God for everything to sustain life, and we learn to lean on Him for our daily sustenance. God is our breath and life, we can't exist without Him.

In verse one of Psalm 104, the writer was overwhelmed with the greatness of God and attempted to express the emotions of his soul saying, *"Bless the Lord, O my soul. O Lord my God, thou art very great; thou art clothed with honour and majesty."* The greatness of God caused the psalmist to probe for words in his vocabulary that could express his true feelings. When we refer to an earthly individual, we often make allowances for their limitations and shortcomings. We try to weigh the person's goodness against their failings and compliment them for being an outstanding individual in spite of their humanity. God however, is pure, holy, and omnipotent. He has no faults, weaknesses, or limitations. In the first book of the Bible, He identified Himself to Abraham as *The Almighty*. In the final book, He likewise identified Himself to John (Gen. 17:1; Rev. 1:8.).

Our God is clothed with majesty and honor. He is indeed deserving of our praise and worship. The word majesty means, "dignity or authority of a sovereign power." There is no darkness in Him because He covers Himself with light as with a garment (Psa.104:2; Jam. 1:17). He is holy and without sin, and the angels around the throne continually cry, "Holy, holy, holy." When Isaiah saw Him in His splendor and glory, it forever changed his life. He said, *"Woe is me! for I am undone; because I am a man of unclean lips, and I dwell in the midst of a people of unclean lips: for mine eyes have seen the King, the Lord of hosts"* (Isa. 6:5).

God Is "Above the Law"

God's presence simultaneously occupies both time and space which allows Him to accomplish His will despite impossibility, naysayers, natural and scientific laws, socioeconomic status, political affiliation, wealth and referential clout. God is "Above the Law" because He made the law. The more something makes no sense, the more logical it appears to God. After all, He said He would use the foolish things of this world to confound the wise.

The "Foolish Things"

> *"But God hath chosen the foolish things of the world to confound the wise; and God hath chosen the weak things of the world to confound the things that are mighty; and base things of the world, and things which are despised, hath God chosen, yea, and things which are not, to bring to nought things that are"* (1Cor. 1: 27-28).

God-gebra focuses on the "foolish things." Things that may have even seemed ridiculous, God deems normative and status quo. For example, it must have seemed very foolish to the people of Jericho or the army of God numbering 600,000 men, to march around Jericho not with AK-47's or assault rifles, but try no weapons at all. Just ram's horns! Talk about unconventional weaponry! What damage or destruction can ram's horns do? To the military strategists and tacticians, this was worse than nonsense. Yet still, the 600,000 men marched in unity and did nothing but blow ram's horns until the time came to shout. When they shouted, the echo of their shout was answered by the roar and crash of the falling walls of the doomed city. The irony of this story is that the method that seemed so idiotic and irrational provided the greatest level of triumph for God's people.

"Foolish things" hath God chosen. It must have seemed very foolish to intelligent men for Christ to tell twelve disciples to feed five thousand men and possibly fifteen thousand women and children with nothing in sight but five loaves and two fishes. They would have laughed you to scorn at Harvard, MIT or any other prestigious institution of higher learning because the likelihood of feeding the masses with such minimal resources is ludicrous and absolute nonsense. Nevertheless at His Word, Jesus' nonsense fed thousands of hungry people and accomplished the intended victory. Who's laughing now?

It must have seemed very foolish for Jesus in choosing illiterate disciples while ignoring Jerusalem with the Sanhedrin (Scholarly Men of the Law) and all its culture. How strange that He purposely ignored Rome during those days. Rome ruled the world, and was in the height of her splendor. The Son of God goes down to the shores of Galilee and handpicks twelve men—unlearned, hard of heart, with broad, brawny hands accustomed to handling oars and tugging at nets. Not many of them were educated. What a foolish thing to put these non-degreed, broken Hebrew speaking men at the head of a movement that was designed and expected to evangelize the world! But when Jesus chose and endowed them with "dunimous power" from heaven, the wisdom of this world was not able to resist the power and anointing with which these men spoke.

The "Weak Things"

God-gebra also focuses on what many consider to be "the weaker things." What was weaker than Moses' rod? God sent Moses against the mightiest empire of the world. At that time, Egypt ruled the world. When Moses was summoned for God's service, he was found on the back side of a mountain feeding sheep. God found him with the smell of the outdoors and just a shepherd's stick, and said, "What is that thou hast in thy hand?" He answered, "A rod." God said, "Throw it on the ground," and when he had done so it became a serpent. Moses was afraid of it, but God said, "Take it by the tail." When he trusted God and grabbed it by the tail, it became a rod again. Moses later stretched forth that rod over Egypt ten times, and ten times the heavens parted as God sent judgment on the Egyptians. With a rod he smote the waters of the Red Sea and they parted. With a rod he struck the rock at Horeb, and a vast river sprang forth, enough for three and a half million famished souls, with all their flocks and herds. God chose "the weak thing."

What was weaker than David's sling? It was just a simple sling that any boy could make. David went down to the brook and picked up five smooth stones, and gained a victory for God that the entire army of Israel had failed to gain. Many times God takes a single man or boy, or girl to win a victory that a whole army of trained soldiers cannot win. God-gebra specializes in using weak things.

What could be weaker than Gideon's three hundred men?

And by the way, what were their weapons? Nothing but lamps and pitchers, and the lamps would not shine until the pitchers were broken. In my opinion, the earthen pitcher represents the majority of Christians today who have never been smashed to pieces by the power of the Holy Ghost. But when the pitchers were broken the light shone out, and three hundred men with nothing but light were enough to scatter the enemy and achieve victory. I doubt very seriously when troops were being deployed to the Middle East that the President of the United States felt comfortable enough executing military strategies with just three hundred men. The American forces currently have thousands of troops involved in "Operation Freedom" in Iraq. But when God wants to fight a battle He delights in getting hold of the smallest nominal thing He can find to bring about the largest margin of victory.

Breaking the Rules

There is an old saying, "rules were made to be broken." If you really study God's ways, you'll find that God is a rule breaker. From the beginning, He has broken rules and defied laws. Even His mere existence is a law breaker. What do I mean? How can anybody or anything just exist without any origin? He breaks the rules by not having a beginning or an ending. As a matter of fact, the Bible opens up by declaring, "In the beginning God..." (Gen. 1:1)

In Matthew 12:1, we pick up on a confrontation in which Jesus is being accused by the Pharisees of defiling the Sabbath (law). Throughout the Bible, Jesus chastised the Pharisees because of their traditional and legalistic views by comparing their relationship to the Sabbath. Keep in mind, the Pharisees had burdened the Sabbath Day with a multitude of detailed observances which turned spiritual ordinances into hypocritical, Spir-RITUAL tactics of "You can't do this! You can't do that!"

Jesus responds to the Pharisees by telling them the story about how David ate the ceremonial shewbread which was against the law.

"Have ye not read what David did, when he was a hungered, and they that were with him; how he entered into the house of God, and did eat the showbread, which was not lawful for him to eat, neither for them which were with him, but only for the priests? But I say unto you, that in this place is one greater than the temple. But if ye had known what this meaneth, I will have mercy, and not sacrifice, ye would not have condemned the guiltless. For the Son of man is Lord even of the sabbath day" (Matt. 12:1).

According to the Mosaic Law in Leviticus 24:9, the bread was only supposed to be eaten by the priests in the Holy Place. Yet, David and his men ate this bread and escaped God's judgment. Why? Their hunger was more important than the keeping of the law.

Jesus declared that He was the Lord of the Sabbath. He was the authority over the Sabbath. He established the rules, and therefore He could break them.

Brothers and sisters, I want you to understand that because of a variety of reasons, too many to name, you may have been excluded from certain things in life. But God will break the rules by applying God-gebra to your situation as He did for David. And the best part is…who can do anything about it? God specializes in granting access to individuals who have been deliberately shut out, left out, rejected or who simply according to some, don't belong and are not worthy to mingle within certain societal circles. God steps in and gives you what others say you shouldn't be able to have. Hallelujah!… What a mighty God we serve!

If God was giving a press conference and a reporter asked Him if He ever broke any rules, I can imagine God saying, "Allow me read my dossier which cites just a few of the ways that I broke "The Rules." I can envision God responding…

- "It was against the rules to have contact with a leper. I did it twice.
- It was against the rules to perform an act of healing on the Sabbath. I broke this rule several times, and at least once I did it in church—to make a point.
- It was against the rules to have contact with tax collectors. I did it anyway.
- It was against the rules to have contact with sinners. I did it my way.

• It was also against rules to consort with Gentiles, and especially Roman soldiers. I not only broke this rule but I even healed the servant of a Roman officer."

If that's not enough evidence to encourage and convince you that God will break the rules on your behalf, God further testifies, "I broke the laws of science when I spoke the sun, firmament, waters, land, grass, stars and living creatures into existence. I broke the laws of physics when I parted the Red Sea and made the sea floor dry enough to walk upon. I broke the laws of energy and combustion when three men were thrown into a fiery furnace and walked out not even having a hair singed or having the scent of fire. I broke the laws of nature when a carnivorous raven brought meat to Elijah and hungry lions refused to eat Daniel. I broke the laws of conception when a virgin conceived a child. I broke the laws of gravity when Peter walked on water. I defied the laws of immortality when a man dead four days walked out of his tomb. I broke the laws of medicine when Peter cut of a man's ear and I mended it without the need for surgery." God concludes His amazing miraculous onslaught by declaring, "I will change your situation and allow the rules to be broken so you can be made whole."

God-gebra is the most excellent explanation one can render to describe God's methodology for imploring these jaw dropping miracles. Let's examine three key aspects of God's unlimited power.

The Characteristic O's of God

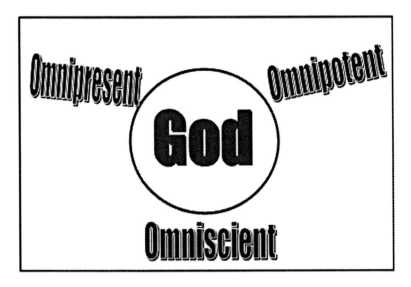

God is Omnipresent, meaning He is everywhere at the same time, for we read: *"Where can I go from Your Spirit? Or where can I flee from Your presence? If I ascend into heaven, You are there; if I make my bed in hell, behold, You are there"* (Psa. 139:7-8).

God is Omnipotent, meaning all-powerful, for we read: *"...'Alleluia! For the Lord God Omnipotent reigns"* (Rev. 19:6).

God is Omniscient, meaning He knows everything, past, present and future, for we read: *"...Lord, You know all things"* (John 21:17).

So when God created the heavens and the earth, He set things in order for the function of life. Even the seas obey His commands (Mark 4:37-41). Birds follow their migratory patterns without a compass and never become lost. The deer and elk follow their instincts for the preservation of the species, and God clothes them with fur to supply their needs for survival. The writer is further convinced of God's power and states, *"The LORD God is my strength, and he will make my feet like hinds' feet, and he will make me to walk upon mine high places"* (Hab. 3:19).

Creation Serves God

The creation of God is subject and submissive to His will. The rivers follow their courses and the oceans stay within their banks. The winds and weather patterns follow the specified commands of God, and the fowls of the air and beasts of the field stay within their habitats and homes. We never see deer trying to climb trees and wolves attempting to fly like wild geese. Fish do not travel on dry ground nor scamper through the forests. God placed specific behavior instincts in all animals, and they adhere to limitations and boundaries that He set upon them.

God is so Awesome…nothing ever catches Him by surprise. He plans everything in minute detail, allowing nothing to escape His attention and care. He attends the funeral of every sparrow that falls and is constantly calculating the number of hairs on our very heads.

All of the elements of nature and animals yield to the awesome power of God. The sun is not supposed to stop in its cycle; but when Joshua prayed, God changed the course of nature where the heavens readjusted at the voice of the Creator (Josh. 10:13).

Water is not supposed to hold an iron ax head on its surface, but it did so at the command of God (2 Kings 6:5-7). God allowed pestilences and droughts to fulfill specific purposes where creation was subject to Him. In the New Testament, water was not supposed to turn to wine, but it did so at the command of God manifested in the flesh (John 2:9-11).

After considering these mind-blowing facts, our cerebral capabilities are rendered helpless to concede that God's power is awe-inspiring and because He can not be limited by height, depth, length or breadth, His power is not bound by limitation. Therefore, every situation is vulnerable to perform His miraculous exploits. In other words, if need be...God will break the rules to bless you!

Chapter 2
The Impossibilities of Life

Now that we have defined the God-gebra concept, in order to completely understand how God uses the principle (a+b+c=x), we must first examine each of the coefficients (a, b, c).

a - An Impossibility

As we dissect the God-gebra equation, the first coefficient a, stands for An Impossibility. What is impossibility? Well, let's first discuss the meaning and definition of the word impossibility.

According to Webster's Dictionary 2006, the definition of Impossibility is as follows:

"Impossibility, A state of being impossible."

• "A certain thing cannot be. (Example), it is impossible that two and two should equal five.

• "There are two kinds of impossibilities; physical and moral. A physical impossibility is considered contrary to the law of nature. A thing is said to be morally impossible, when in itself it is possible, but attended with difficulties or circumstances which give it the appearance of being impossible."

Although Webster describes two types of impossibilities, I want to focus on the physical aspect of impossibility. Ironically, when giving us the definition of impossibility, Webster's states," It is impossible that two and two should make five." However, this is the type of problem that is most accurately solved by God-gebra. Why? Because there is no possible way that the numerical values of 2+2 should ever equal = 5. But with God-gebra the impossibility can be a reality. Let's examine further.

In the thirty second chapter of the Book of Jeremiah, the seventeenth verse, Jeremiah is in a "shock and awe" state because of God's power to transform impossibility into reality. He responds with great respect and wonder by declaring:

> *"Ah Lord GOD! behold, thou hast made the heaven and the earth by thy great power and stretched out arm, and there is nothing too hard for thee"* (Jer. 32:17).

Jeremiah had received the revelation that God, in His awesome splendor, has an uncanny ability to use situations that defy logic and the laws of nature, and now allows these re-defined rules to work against themselves and produce what could best be described as a miraculous manifestation called "God-gebra".

Like Jeremiah, many of us need to gain a more intimate understanding of the awesome power of God. I believe there are situations in our lives currently that could benefit from us getting a more complete revelation of just how majestic and mighty the power of God is. Keep in mind, that oft times in order to get a more acute revelatory prospective of God, we have to be placed in situations of impossibility, where technically speaking, there is no way out!

Let's examine this concept further through the eyes of three Hebrew Men:

The story unfolds as King Nebuchadnezzar erected a golden image (Dan. 3:1). In arrogance the king makes a decree that every man that hears the sound of various instruments fall down and worship the golden image. Contained in this decree was a clause that stated, anyone who fails to bow down and worship the image would be thrown into a fiery furnace (Dan. 3:10-11). The accusers brought to King Nebachadnezzar's attention that Shadrach, Meshach and Abednego defied his decree by refusing to bow and worship the golden image. The king offers the Hebrew men an opportunity to recant their decision by asking them, "Who is that God that shall deliver you out of my hands?" The three men as they faced the possibility of certain death by being burned alive, replied, *"If it be so, our God who we serve is able to deliver us from the burning fiery furnace, and he will deliver us out of thine hand, o king"* (Dan. 3:17). The king was infuriated by their response and commanded the furnace be heated 7 times hotter than normal. And if that wasn't enough, to add insult to injury, the king commanded the men to be bound before being cast into the fiery furnace.

First of all, what is the significance of binding these men when they were probably going to die instantly (like the men that simply opened the door to the furnace in Daniel 3:22) because of the intensified heat of the furnace? Secondly, why did the king command the "Mightiest Men" in his army to bind them when death once again seemed imminent? (Dan. 3:20)

I believe the answer to this question stems from King Nebachadnezzar's desire to emphasize the state of *Total Impossibility* and certain doom of the three Hebrew men. God will often allow us to be placed in a cliffhanger. A position where it seems we will suffer certain demise at the hand of our adversary. The situation of impossibility becomes so severely evident and any outlook that provides a glimmer of hope for a rescue would *have to be* considered divine and God ordained. God will then apply God-gebra, his formula of choice for balancing impossible situations. Let's see how God deals with Impossibility of the Hebrew men.

As the story concludes, the three Hebrew men are subsequently cast in the fiery furnace. Faced with impossible odds of survival and certain death, God delivered them as they came out of the furnace unharmed, and without even the smell of fire (Dan. 3:26-27).

Here is a paradigm shift, don't become stressful but rejoice and be comforted when facing life's impossibilities (1 Pet. 4:12-13). Be encouraged! God has not forgotten you. In order for others around us to see God and believe on Him, He allows our tribulations to appear bleak, just as He did with the three Hebrew men—only to turn the tide at His appointed time. Remember, when facing impossibility, let God's rhetorical response to troubling situations be a comfort to you.

> Behold, I am the LORD, the God of all flesh: *is there any thing too hard for me?* (Jer. 32:27)

Personal Impossibilities

In John 9:1-3, Jesus is traveling with His disciples. *"And as Jesus passed by, he saw a man which was blind from his birth. And his disciples asked him, saying, Master, who did sin, this man, or his parents, that he was born blind? Jesus answered, Neither hath this man sinned, nor his parents: but that the works of God should be made manifest in him.*

In this text, Jesus is teaching and emphasizing to His disciples that every situation of impossibility is not a result or consequence of sin. Jesus quickly renders a closing statement that responds to their inquisition and answers the proverbial question, why? Jesus responds emphatically, "That God might be glorified in impossibilities."

Two important aspects learned from this narrative.

1. The disciples received additional sight through revelation of a blind man's healing.

2. The blind man received his sight via personal revelation and can testify to the awesome power of the Almighty God resulting from a situation of personal impossibility.

A Personal Impossibility

Speaking of personal impossibility, I can remember a time when was growing up and I asked my mother, "Why did you name me Ivan?" She responded, "Your name is synonymous with God's goodness. It means God's Gift." She said, "Let me tell you a story:

When I was younger, I was diagnosed with a lung disease called sarcoidosis. Sarcoidosis is the abnormal formation of fiber-like scar tissue in the lung. This disease distorts the structure of the lungs and can interfere with breathing. This disease had become so concentrated in my lung, I can remember the doctors' saying that I would probably never be able to have children. I can remember seeing other mothers enjoy the happiness and fulfillment of their children and thinking, 'Lord I know the doctors have declared this an impossibility, but I serve and put my trust in you.'" She went on to say, that there were many nights that she would cry out to the Lord to hear and grant her request for a child.

In 1970, her prayers were answered when she discovered after many unsuccessful attempts, that she was with child. Her celebratory jubilation was quickly smothered by uncertainty and doubt. Because as soon as she realized she was pregnant, the doctors began to tell her that because of the severity of the disease, she could very well jeopardize her health or place the unborn child in harms way. As my mother explained further, I could see her eyes begin to gradually water, increasing with each portion of this story. She stopped several times to gather her composure until she was able to muster enough strength to continue. She said it felt like she was between a rock and a hard place. The situation had gotten to a point where she contemplated giving up but she had come too far to turn back now.

My mother began to smile as she recalled the last subsequent events of this story. She hugged me and said, "When I felt I had come to my lowest point, I could feel God strengthen and prepare me for the awesome results that I believed by faith would happen. Suddenly, I remember the doctors saying, 'it's a Boy! It's a Boy!' The wonder and amazement that filled Harper Grace Hospital on July 27, 1970 at 10:46 am, was nothing short of spectacular."

My mother concluded the story by saying, "Son, the doctors had been proven wrong, sarcoidosis had been rendered helpless and God in His awesome splendor had done something only He could perform." My mother wrapped her arms around me and said, "Son, I Love You and always remember that you are God's gift to me; and in life, your circumstances are never over, only until God says there are over!"

As I recall my conversation with my mother, I am reminded yet again of the account in John 9:1-3. My mother had done no wrong by desiring to have a child. But instead, she was selected by God to give others, like the disciples, a more insightful revelation. She became a revelatory instrument, like the blind man, to show forth the power and majesty of God.

Personal Impossibility provides yet another backdrop for God to apply God-gebra to make the unattainable a very present reality.

More out of Little

We live in a society obsessed with the mindset that views material possessions as the primary marker of success. Quests for prosperity rather than fulfillment through contentment have become the new mantra by which many self evaluate and chart their course for eternity. We further evidence this notion in a variety of ways defined throughout our culture.

Let me give you a few examples:

- The Majority Rules (Law of the Land)
- The More, The Merrier (Colloquialism)
- He Who Has The Gold Rules (Colloquialism)
- Show Me The Money (Movie-Jerry McGuire)
- Get Rich, or Die Trying (Movie-50 Cent)
- Bling! Bling! (Culture Slang for Material Wealth)

These examples highlight the degree to which our society has deteriorated by taken its dependence from God and placing it within the confines of "popular vote" or "material aggrandizement and self promotion".

Historically, God has always done more with less. And no matter how society evolves to further suggest that materialism is a substitute for the favor God, it is just not so. God has always astonished many by His ability to utilize and empower the least, the underdog, the youngest, the smallest, the blind, the cripple and the poor to accomplish His will. Insufficiency becomes yet another God-gebra calling card as God places His distinguishing mark on life's situations.

Insufficiency Moves God

Insufficiency, most often referred to as lack, has a negative connotation associated with it because by definition, it implies that you are "A Day Late and A Dollar Short". And further more, it emphatically concludes, that your resources have been utterly exhausted. But it is in this type of situation that God finds Himself God-gebraically working to alter your current state of affairs.

I am reminded of the account where Jesus fed four thousand people. He asked the disciplines, *"How many loaves have ye?"* They replied, *"seven, and a few little fishes"* (Matt. 15:34). Even though there were only seven loaves of bread and a few fishes, Jesus inexplicably fed four thousand people and had fragments left over that amounted to seven baskets of food.

Another time, Jesus was amidst five thousand men including women and children. He asks the disciples, how much food did they have, and they replied," *Five loaves, and two fishes*" (Matt. 14:17). Note how the God-gebra principle is at work in this situation. Jesus has more people to feed but less food to work with. When He fed four thousand people he had seven loaves of bread and a few fishes. With over five thousand people to feed, He had five loaves and two fishes. Jesus astonishingly fed five thousand plus people with fewer resources, but God-gebra reveals that He had more left over feeding the five thousand collectively, than He did in feeding the four thousand. After feeding five thousand, there were 12 baskets of food leftover (Matt. 14:20). This breaks down God-gebraically to reveal that... More People + Less food = More Leftover!

Paradoxically, God will utilize your insufficiency to multiply your blessing and do more in your situation with less. God specializes in utilizing what you currently have (even if it's minimal) by blessing it, breaking it and making it meat for the Master's use.

El Shaddai: The God of More than Enough

El Shaddai is one of seven Hebrew names of which God revealed Himself to Israel throughout the Old Testament. The name El Shaddai in Hebrew means "All Sufficient One." He is the God of more than enough. But what exactly does this mean? It means He is our *All Sufficient God* and causes what seems most likely to be described as a shortage or deficiency, to continually produce results without explanation or likelihood of ending.

In the Book of 1Kings, Chapter 17, Elijah has just completed an individual course in God-gebra 101. He has just experienced how God can take the foolish things of this world and confound the wise (1 Cor. 1:27-28). Earlier in this chapter, God told Elijah to settle down for dinner by the Brook at Cherith. There he would be sumptuously served by tuxedo clad waiters at a five star restaurant. No! But rather by ravens, who by the way are carnivorous by nature. As we stated in Chapter 1, one key principle of God-gebra is that it is most effectively applied when pitted against the laws of nature. *"The ravens brought him bread and meat in the morning, and bread and meat in the evening; and he drank from the brook"* (1Kings 17:6).

One of the main contributors to Elijah's success in this narrative is his obedience. How many times has God spoken to our spirits and said, go to certain place or do a certain thing but because the request appeared illogical to us, we disregarded the command. We said to ourselves, "This makes no sense." But because of Elijah's obedience, God proved to him that He was El-Shaddai: More Than Enough.

Some might suggest, "After all, this is Elijah, God's prophet and I am just an ordinary person." But guess what? God's Word is no respecter of person or personalities. It (His Word) responds by completing the task at hand after being activated by individuals who decide to obey. If you are experiencing a financial shortage or perhaps you are contemplating whether to pay your bills or pay your tithes, God's Word says that the tithe is the tenth of your increase (Num. 18:26). God also instructs us to, *"Bring ye all the tithes into the storehouse, that there may be meat in mine house, and PROVE ME NOW HEREWITH, SAITH THE LORD OF HOSTS, if I will not open you the windows of heaven, and pour you out a blessing, that there shall not be room enough to receive it"* (Mal. 3:10). In other words, God is saying, "If you want to see if I am more than enough, be obedient and prove me!"

In the Book of 2 Kings, there is a desperate woman who puts God's "prove me" challenge to the test. The story unfolds as a creditor threatens to take a widow's two sons as slaves if she didn't repay the debt owed (2 Kings 4:1). Does this sound familiar to anyone? Anybody have a debt that seems insurmountable and overwhelming? The widow, like many of us, worried and not knowing what to do, she petitions the prophet Elisha for help. He responds by asking her, *"What hast thou in the house?"* (2 Kings 4:2) She replied, *"Nothing, except a pot of oil."* Elisha told her to go and borrow vessels from her neighbors, pour the oil into the vessels and sell them to pay off the debt. Let's be honest, this makes very little sense. I can imagine the widow thinking, "This man wants me to borrow again. This is how I got into this financial quagmire, because of borrowing." She probably thought to herself, "Even if I borrow the neighbors' pots, I don't have enough oil to fill all the vessels." But nevertheless, at the Word of God through the prophet Elijah, the woman obeyed. Obedience activated the power of God (God-gebra) and the widow was set free from the bondage of debt and the dread of losing her sons.

Acting in obedience and not allowing human logic to be a hindrance, will propel God-gebra into effect and allow you to witness first hand, why God is known as El-Shaddai: The God of More Than Enough.

Chapter 3
Beyond Hope

As we began to further dissect the God-gebra equation, a quick recap reminds us that the first coefficient a stands for a Impossibility. For the next component of the God-gebra concept (a+b+c=x), we will study the coefficient b which represents Beyond Hope.

b - (Beyond Hope)

> *"I wait for the Lord, my soul doth wait, and in his word do I hope"* (Psalm 130:5).

Times of distress are common in the lives of the believer. Situations arise simply because we are part of this world. However, as children of God, we have an assurance that the Lord has everything under control even when conditions seem out of control. By crying out to Him in prayer, God has given us a release valve to discharge the pressure of circumstances by making our requests known to Him who is the author and finisher of our faith (Heb. 12:2).

We live in a society where people are more comfortable taking their own lives amidst turmoil and uncertainty than to call on a righteous God that ardently says, *"He will never leave us or forsake us"* (Heb 13:5). We have been conditioned and trained to trust alternative measures like finances, education, and political reformation and have neglected to put the healing and consoling power of Jesus Christ to the test.

God has favored us by allowing us the privilege to seek His help in the hour of need. He is concerned about every aspect of our lives. God wants us to have faith in Him and a sure hope; although different, these two qualities are closely related. Matthew Henry Commentary states, *"Faith respects the promise, hope the thing promised. Faith is the evidence, hope the expectation."* The character of faith and hope are both essential tools in the building strategy of the Christian walk.

Ever been in a situation that appeared to have No Way Out? The situation appeared so despairing that it caused you to give up hope toward believing the condition could be remedied. This is nothing but a trick of the enemy. The influences of Satan often tell us subliminally that there is no way God could ever deliver you because your situation has deteriorated and shortly thereafter, your hope along with it. You are caught between a proverbial "rock and a hard place." The longer you wait, the more hopeless the situation looks. Until finally you come to the conclusion that my situation is Beyond Hope. This is ironically the situation the Children of Israel faced while being delivered from Egypt in the Book of Exodus.

After Moses brought the last plague upon Pharaoh and upon Egypt, God said, *"afterwards he will let you go"* (Ex. 11:1). The story unfolds as Pharaoh ultimately let's the people go only to later decide to pursue them (Ex. 14:3). He utilizes all his resources, horses and chariots and his army to pursue them with the goal of re-enslaving God's people. In John 8:36, the scripture tells us, *"If the Son (Jesus Christ) therefore shall make you free, ye shall be free indeed."* God had given the decree that the children of Israel would be freed from the yoke of bondage. As Pharaoh and his military entourage drew closer, the people began to fear and complain.

> *"And when Pharaoh drew nigh, the children of Israel lifted up their eyes, and, behold, the Egyptians marched after them; and they were sore afraid: and the children of Israel cried out unto the Lord. And they said to Moses, Because there were no graves in Egypt, hast thou taken us away to die in the wilderness? Wherefore hast thou dealt thus with us, carry us forth out of Egypt?"* (Ex. 14:10-11)

The Children of Israel began to see their dilemma much the way we tend to view ours, bleak and Beyond Hope. So much so, that the children of Israel verbally attack Moses and proclaimed that they would rather turn back and reconnect with the same hopeless, unfruitful, horrific example of degradation rather than to receive the promise and trust the awesome power of God which has already delivered them.

> *"Is not this the word that we did tell thee in Egypt, saying, let us alone, that we may serve the Egyptians? For it had been better for us to serve the Egyptians, than that we should die in the wilderness"* (Ex. 14:12).

Moses responds with the same rebuttal we should respond with and that's simply, *"Fear ye not, stand still and see the salvation of the Lord, which he will shew you to day: for the Egyptians you have seen today, ye shall see no more for ever. The Lord shall fight for you and ye shall hold your peace"* (Ex. 14:13-14).

Let's rewind the story to evaluate the current details:

1. Moses brings the last plague (First born will die)
2. Pharaoh decides to release the Children of Israel
3. God hardens Pharaoh's Heart
4. Pharaoh decides to recapture the Children of Israel
5. Pharaoh and his Army draw closer
6. Israel fears death at Pharaoh's hand
7. Israel tells Moses they should have stayed in Egypt
8. Israel is sandwiched between Pharaoh's Army and the Red Sea (Beyond Hope)

9. Moses tells Israel: "Fear Not, Stand Still and the Lord will fight for you"
10. God delivers the Children of Israel and defeats their enemy

Many of us who face situations which appear to be Beyond Hope find ourselves at step# 8. God has allowed certain situations to place us between "Our Past and His Promise." But hopelessness has caused us to distrust God and look for other alternatives to unlock our present bondage.

Moses gives the children of Israel the God-gebra principle that will transform their Beyond Hope psyche (step #8) into a mind frame of victory and deliverance found at steps 9 & 10. He tells them, *"Fear Not, Stand Still and the Lord will fight for you."* The Children of Israel's victory was predicated and revealed in their ability to stand on God's Word, not by taking matters into their own hands. In other words, their blessing was at a Stand Still. (Hallelujah!)

It is with this battle cry that I encourage you as well. Hopelessness is just one of the many ways the enemy will coerce you to give up so you will abort and forfeit the plan of God for your life and ultimately, never receive the blessing that God has in store. However, there is a balm in Gilead (Jer. 46:11). God-gebra works most efficaciously when applied to predicaments and circumstances defined as being Beyond Hope. God-gebra is specifically designed to strip away doubt and exploit hopeless situations by allowing them to catapult us into destiny and fulfillment of purpose.

Hope-Full or Hope-Less

Ask yourself a simple question. Are you Hope-full or Hope-less? Interestingly enough, you must stake claim to one or the other because one cannot occupy both places simultaneously. Why? You might ask. Maintaining an attitude of being hope-full (full of hope) means there is an absence of hopelessness (did you get that?). Likewise, if you are hope-less, you have a proclivity to lack the perspective necessary to see positive outcome in the midst of challenging situations.

Do you view challenges to be opportunities to excel or excuses for failure? I recall one of my instructors who used to motivate the class by saying, "What you see depends on where you sit!" I remember wondering, "What in the world does this mean." Several years later, I received the revelation of the colloquialism. It means, "Attitude determines Altitude."

Your outlook during stressful situations is directly related to the outcome. In other words, our hope-fullness should be dependant upon a God who has unlimited resources to meet needs regardless of how it looks. Considering the fact that He cannot lie or fail, we should find comfort in knowing if we wait patiently with hope-fullness, God will reward our efforts in His time.

Hope in Times of Distress

It has been clinically proven that most individuals will lose hope when placed in circumstances of distress over an extended period of time. Let's statistically test our hypothesis.

The data suggests:

- Depression (Hopelessness) is the 3rd leading cause of death for 15-19 aged youngsters
- There is a 300% increase in suicides over the last 30 years
- 19 adolescents die each day, 5000-7000 young people each year end their own lives
- Hopelessness & Depression is a common antecedent to suicide.
- Sociologists tell us that 20,000 to 50,000 young adult suicides in the United States were all preceded by Depression and Hopelessness

According to this data, the world we live in suffers daily from a lack of hope and because of this malady, many find it easier to commit suicide rather than to believe or hope that through practical alternatives their situations can be improved.

I am reminded of the psalmist who had reached a low point in his life when he wrote, *"Out of the depths have I cried unto thee, O Lord"* (Psa. 130:1). He was not just experiencing a minor setback he was at a point of deep despair. Has anyone ever been there? I have.

There are times in our lives when opposition and turmoil

appear to have the upper hand. It seems as if everywhere we turn the walls of anguish and disappointment appear to be closing in. I can remember the time the disciples were in a desperate situation and the Lord encouraged their hope by saying:

> *"I am the vine, ye are the branches: He that abideth in me, and*
> *I in him, the same bringeth forth much fruit: for without me ye*
> *can do nothing"* (John 15:5).

Peter came to the realization that many of us need to conclude, *"Lord, to whom shall we go? Thou hast the words of eternal life"* (John 6:68).

Peter's revelation should encourage us in the fact that although we have needs that have placed us between promise and fulfillment, God has the ability to meet our needs according to His riches in glory which are inexhaustible. God's storehouses of blessings are never depleted. God can meet the world's many needs and still have time to tuck each bird in at night and set the alarm clock for the sun to get up each morning; while He oversees the day to day operations of the cosmos. What a Mighty God we serve!

Because only God sits on the circle of the earth, we do not always see things as He does. We tend to view our difficulties from a human perspective. These difficulties usually manifest themselves in three major areas: Financial, Physical and Spiritual.

1. Financial Hope

Economic situations over the last several years have caused institutions that were once considered "untouchable" and secure to now crumble at the face of financial deterioration. Here in Michigan for example, multi-national automotive corporations like the Big Three (Ford, General Motors and Chrysler) are downsizing and thousands of people are facing mammoth layoffs. As a result, the residential foreclosure rate in Michigan is the highest in the nation. Detroit, the largest city in Michigan, has received the dubious honor of being one of "The Poorest Cities in America." Thirty two percent of its inhabitants live below the poverty level. The economic plight here in Michigan is so bleak that the only city/state with a worse financial and economic outlook is New Orleans, Louisiana the site of hurricane Katrina.

Christians are not immune or unaffected by these conditions, but we have a "hope" that provides piece of mind despite demoralizing circumstances. I am reminded of the scripture that says, *"I have been young and now I am old; yet I have never seen the righteous forsaken, nor his seed begging bread"* (Psa. 37:25).

Jesus also encouraged the disciples by stating, *"Therefore I say unto you, Take no thought for your life, what ye shall eat, or what ye shall drink; nor yet for your body, what ye shall put on. Is not the life more than meat, and the body than raiment? Behold the fowls of the air: for they sow not, neither do they reap, nor gather into barns; yet your heavenly Father feedeth them. Are ye not much better than they? Which of you by taking thought can add one cubit unto his stature? And why take ye thought for raiment?*

Consider the lilies of the field, how they grow; they toil not, neither do they spin: and yet I say unto you, That even Solomon in all his glory was not arrayed like one of these. Wherefore, if God so clothe the grass of the field, which today is, and tomorrow is cast into the oven, shall he not much more clothe you, O ye of little faith? Therefore take no thought, saying, What shall we eat? or, What shall we drink? or, Wherewithal shall we be clothed? (For after all these things do the Gentiles seek:) for your heavenly Father knoweth that ye have need of all these things. But seek ye first the kingdom of God, and his righteousness; and all these things shall be added unto you. Take therefore no thought for the morrow: for the morrow shall take thought for the things of itself. Sufficient unto the day is the evil thereof" (Matt. 6:25-34).

During this exhortation, Jesus re-emphasizes the fact that we should be comforted in the midst of adversity. Jesus further explains that the birds of the air have no permanent address and if they could talk, could not tell you today where they are going to be tomorrow. Jesus further outlines that if these fowls of the air flourish without having "hope" and are not concerning themselves about their daily needs, how much more should we as Christians be reassured that no matter what financial situation befalls us, God will meet every need.

On December 18, 2006, one week before Christmas, I was told by my company after seven loyal years of service, that I would no longer have a job because of budget cuts and restructuring initiatives. As I considered this news, I thought to my self, I have always been faithful to my responsibilities and was regularly rewarded as a "Top Performer" by the organization. I further contemplated the fact that my wife and I recently built a beautiful home and I have bills that need to be paid so I can continue to sustain the lifestyle to which we had become accustomed. I began to ponder about my future and wonder, "How am I going to continue providing for my beautiful wife and two small children?" I can remember the look of uncertainty in my wife's eyes; although she never let on to her discomfort, I could feel her coming unglued when faced with the probability of us losing it all.

As I write this paragraph, today is June 14, 2007 and I can humbly say that God has met my family's every need throughout my being laid off. There has never been a time where God allowed us to go hungry or receive a shut off notice because of payment delinquency. Now, things are tight and I don't have the liberty and freedom to spend as I did previously, but God is teaching me that if I trust Him to meet my needs, He is faithful to perform.

2. Physical Hope

The scriptures contain many accounts of how Jesus healed all manner of diseases. As the great physician, He caused the blind to see; the deaf to hear; the palsied, withered or maimed to be restored; lepers to be cleansed; and unclean spirits to be cast out. Jesus specialized in curing all maladies and according to the scriptures, every person He healed of these physical ailments was "made whole" (Matt. 14:36; Mark 6:56; John 5:9).

In most cases if you ask a Christian if they believe that Jesus healed the lepers or open blinded eyes, they will respond emphatically, "Yes!" However, if we were to rephrase the question to inquire whether they believe Jesus can heal their current situation, the answer may not be as emphatic. Why? Because often times it becomes easier for us to believe the God of the Bible but lack the hope to believe He will perform in our lives. The Bible explains,

> *"But my God shall supply your need according to his riches in glory by Christ Jesus"* (Phil. 4:19).

God desires for us to prosper even as our souls doth prosper (3 John 1:2). This simply means that God wants us to have the best that He can give us. God wants to go beyond just the material manifestations of His love to include being healed completely and functioning without hindrance in our physical bodies. I remember when Jesus passed a blind man on the road and the apostles asked who sinned this man or his parents? Jesus responded,

> *"Neither hath this man sinned, nor his parents: but that the works of God should be made manifest in him"* (John 9:3).

God gets the glory when we live an abundant life and He will do everything in His power to meet our physical needs. Having hope in the midst of the physical infirmities can only be remedied by the Holy One who specializes in manifesting deliverance in the hour of despair.

3. Spiritual Hope

One of the ways in which our society has shown a loss of hope is by attempting to cure spiritual diseases with natural remedies. It would be analogous to placing a band aid on a broken arm. Our society has become content with labeling spiritual diseases such as lust, with various medical descriptions. Lust could be medically interpreted as suffering from a veracious insatiable appetite for the opposite sex brought on by a lack of positive relational interactions throughout ones life. It doesn't matter how you choose to define it, the prognosis is still sin. And sin can never be forgiven or washed away by simply taking a couple of pills twice a day.

As a people that were created in the image and likeness of God, we can never eradicate the carnal, sinful nature of our flesh by sweeping it under the rug of medical phraseology which seeks to release us from blame and provides further evidence of our inability to crucify our flesh. We have sought to replace God with many man-made substitutes from which we feel we can derive some self sustaining hope without fear of accountability and commitment.

Contrary to popular belief, only the undeniable redemptive blood of Jesus can wash away sin and provide spiritual hope in times of distress. This cleansing process can only be performed by first repenting and being baptized in the name of Jesus, and receiving the Holy Spirit according to Acts 2:38. As we receive the Holy Spirit we are now empowered to operate with spiritual hope which enables us to lead others to follow the same pattern.

Keep Hope Alive

"Keep Hope Alive" is a very familiar slogan made famous by the renowned civil rights activist Rev. Jesse Jackson. This mantra has been the motivation for a people to rise above their political, social and economic plight to seek solace and comfort under the revolutionizing power of a phrase dominated by the word "Hope".

Upon further study and revelation, I discovered that the contrary takes place. What is the contrary? Well, in actuality, it is HOPE that keeps us alive. The scriptures tell us in Romans 8:24, *"For we are saved by hope: but hope that is seen is not hope: for what a man seeth, why doth he yet hope for?"*

So when you really examine the characteristics of hope, one of them speaks to the ability to save or rescue individuals from their predicament because the hope possessed during situations of hopelessness cause them to lean on a hope-Full God.

The second aspect of hope that I found to be enlightening is the fact that the scripture speaks volumes to us by revealing that "hope that is seen, is not hope."

How does one see hope? Well, I would like to interpret further by stating for the record that I believe that how you see your way out of a situation (hope-Full) will depend on your faith in the Almighty God. In other words, when you are faced with obstacles and you can see or predict the outcome, this would not be considered hope. Why? Let me give you an example. If I received a shut off notice in the mail and I have the money to pay the bill, where is the hope in this situation? Hope in this example has been suffocated by the blanket of self sufficiency and my own "resourcefulness". However, if I lack the funding to meet the financial obligation, then I am compelled to lean on the God-gebraic arms of God and believe thru my faith that He will make a way of escape. During my wait I find that my faith in God has increased because when human options were exhausted the only logical conclusion to the matter is God-gebra. So while you are waiting on your manifestation, put your Hope in God.

Today, if your find yourself waiting on the promises of God and it seems like you are losing hope, be encouraged and strengthened with the following paraphrased scriptures and remember, *Hope is Keeping You Alive!*

Hope

"In His name the Gentiles will hope" (Matt. 12:21)

"Grace...exalt in hope of the glory of God"(Rom. 5:2).

"Hope does not disappoint, because the love of God is poured within our hearts through the Holy Spirit (Rom. 5:5).

"May the God of hope fill you with all joy and peace…that you may abound in hope, by the power of the Holy Spirit" (Rom. 15:13).

"If we have only hoped in Christ in this life, we are to be pitied" (I Cor. 15:19).

"Having such a hope, we use great boldness in our speech" (2 Cor. 3:12).

"We through the Spirit, by faith, are waiting for the hope of righteousness" (Gal. 5:5).

"You may know what is the hope of His calling" (Eph. 1:18).

"Continue in the faith…not moved away from the hope of the gospel" (Col. 1:23).

"Christ in you, the hope of glory" (Col 1:27).

"Christ Jesus who is our hope" (1Tim 1:1).

"We have fixed our hope on the living God who is the Savior of all men" (I Tim. 4:10).

"The hope of eternal life" (Titus 1:2).

"Looking for the blessed hope and the appearing of the glory of Christ" (Titus 2:13).

"There is a bringing in of a better hope" (Heb. 7:19).

"Born again to a living hope through the resurrection of Jesus Christ" (I Pet. 1:3).

"Fix your hope completely on the grace to be brought to you at the revelation of Jesus Christ" (I Pet. 1:13).

"Ready to make a defense…for the hope that is in you" (I Pet. 3:15).

"Every one who has this hope on Him purifies himself" (I John 3:3).

Satan is the king of hopelessness and a pathological liar. He has no hope of redemption and seeks to recruit others to adopt his hopelessness for their own lives. We need not believe the devil's lies, since we have every hope of redemption and forgiveness through faith in Jesus Christ!

Chapter 4
Certain Measure of Faith

As we prepare to discuss the third layer of the God-gebra equation, a quick recap reminds us that the first coefficient a, stands for An Impossibility. The second coefficient b is described as Beyond Hope. As part of the third component of the God-gebra concept (a+b+c=x), we will study the coefficient c, which represents a Certain Measure of Faith.

c - (Certain Measure of Faith)

In chapters two and three we investigated certain circumstances in which God deploys God-gebra to alter situational outcomes in order to reposition our lives. Our next ingredient, which is faith, is crucial to this concept. As a matter of fact, if faith is not activated, it renders all other components helpless to perform their tasks. But with faith the God-gebra principle operates in the lives of believers like a fine-tuned well oiled machine. There is absolutely nothing you can't do when you exercise your faith.

F (Full) A (assurance) I (in) T (the) H (hope)

In the last chapter, while studying the significance of having hope, we determined that hope and faith are closely related. As a matter of fact, whenever you see faith in scripture, hope is usually not far behind. Let me show you…

> *"Therefore, having been justified by FAITH, we have peace with God through our Lord Jesus Christ, through whom also we have access by FAITH into this grace in which we stand, and rejoice in HOPE of the glory of God. And not only that, but we also glory in tribulations, knowing that tribulation produces perseverance; and perseverance, character; and character, HOPE. Now HOPE does not disappoint, because the love of God has been poured out in our hearts by the Holy Spirit who was given to us. For when we were still without strength, in due time Christ died for the ungodly"* (Rom. 5:1-6, NKJV).

> *"FAITH is the substance of things HOPED for…"* (Heb 11:1).

If hope is closely related to faith, how do we tell them apart?

Faith and hope are tools we need in order to walk in victory over sin. Faith is like an ATM card to God's Kingdom. By faith in Jesus Christ, we have access to God and the promises He has made in His Word to us. Additionally, through faith, we have peace with God and the hope of experiencing and enjoying the magnificence of God.

Standing in faith, we can endure trials and tribulations knowing that a Godly hope will result. This hope will not let us down, because it comes from God. God has poured out His love in our hearts in the form of the Holy Spirit, who is a guarantor of our inheritance as children of God. The Spirit strengthens our faith and bolsters our hope as we strive to walk in the newness of life in Jesus Christ (Rom. 6:4).

The devil loves to attack and destroy our hope whenever he can. If our faith is weak, our hope will easily fall when trials and tribulations come our way. The devil's primary weapon to destroy our faith is doubt. Trials and tribulations are often secondary weapons used in conjunction with doubt. The combination of these weapons can be overwhelming for us if we are not firmly grounded in our faith in God.

To further understand the distinction between hope and faith, ask yourself a couple of key questions:

Question #1: Can you have Hope without Faith? The answer is yes.

Question #2: Can you have Faith without Hope? The answer is No. Here's why?

By definition, faith is described as the substance of things hoped for and the evidence of things not seen. So, I believe it's possible to have hope without faith, but not faith without hope. Further clarification suggests that having faith is all encompassing of possessing hope as well. Second Corinthians 10:15 corroborates this theory by stating, *"Not boasting of things without our measure, that is, of other men's labours; but having hope, WHEN your faith is increased, that we shall be enlarged by you according to our rule abundantly."* Look at it this way, faith is the combo meal that upgrades you to receive hope at no extra charge.

> *"Through faith we understand that the worlds were framed by the word of God, so that things which are seen were not made of things which do appear"* (Heb. 11:3).

To have faith is to see things in the spiritual world, before they become visible, or physical. It is not just a simple knowledge, it is true wisdom. "Faith is the eyes of the spirit."

Hope is to believe that something you desire will happen. Hope combined with faith gives you power to change your life and the lives of those around you.

Faith may be applied differently depending on the circumstances. The following definitions describe three ways in which faith can be activated in the lives of the believer.

These three definitions are:

1. Faith involves trusting God rather than relying on conventional means for something you need.
2. Faith is completely trusting God for an outcome even when that trust incurs personal risk which could otherwise be avoided.
3. Faith consists of trusting God for an outcome which is impossible through human effort irrespective of the willingness to incur risk.

What does the BIBLE say about faith?

"Now faith is the substance of things hoped for, the evidence of things NOT SEEN" (Heb 11:1).

"For I say, through the grace given unto me, to every man that is among you, not to think of himself more highly than he ought to think; but to think soberly, according as God hath dealt to EVERY MAN the measure of faith" (Rom. 12:3).

"Then touched he their eyes, saying, ACCORDING TO YOUR FAITH BE IT UNTO YOU" (Matt. 9:29).

"But WITHOUT FAITH IT IS IMPOSSIBLE TO PLEASE HIM: for he that cometh to God must believe that he is, and that he is a rewarder of them that diligently seek him" (Heb. 11:6).

"He (Abraham) staggered not at the promise of God through unbelief; but was STRONG IN FAITH" (Rom. 4:20).

So based upon the Bible's testimony, we can formulate five important truths regarding Faith. The 5 IT'S of Faith are:

1. "You can't see it"
2. "Every man (and woman) has it"
3. "You can have anything with it"
4. "You can't please God without it"
5. "You grow stronger by exercising it"

The following illustration depicts the results of exercising your faith:

"Faith Sustained"
By Exercise

Resistance makes You stronger

The only way to grow stronger in Faith is to use it

Exercising your Faith will allow you to move bigger mountains

Exercising your faith will allow you to develop muscles that you never knew existed and in doing so, you will begin to see manifestations that you have never seen before.

Hebrews Chapter 11, "The Hall of Faith"

The "Hall of Fame" is a type of museum established for the purposes of honoring individuals of noteworthy achievement in a certain field. For example, there is a football Hall of Fame in Canton, Ohio. There, you will find the encased shoes that Jim Brown wore when he set the single season NFL rushing record. On display, you will also find the actual football that Terry Bradshaw of the Pittsburgh Steelers used to throw multiple touchdowns with in the Super Bowl.

Many athletes begin athletic careers perfecting their craft at the sport of choice with the ultimate goal of winning championships, but dreaming all the while of being inducted into the "Hall of Fame." As a matter of fact, you may have been considered a perennial all star at your particular sport, but that does not automatically qualify you to be inducted into the "Hall of Fame." Ironically, many athletes are currently waiting to receive their place in history amongst the best to have ever played their respective sport.

Similarly, Hebrews the eleventh chapter memorializes the amazing efforts of those who excelled likewise in Christendom.

They did not hit over 700 homeruns or have a lifetime batting average of 400, or even score 84 points in a basketball game during their career, but the qualifying criteria for their induction was the level of "faith" they exhibited throughout their lifetime of walking with God. The Bible gives certain credence and noteworthiness to their monumental feats of excellence but ironically, many of these people were not born with phenomenal talent. Unlike superstar athletes, these inductees were ordinary people with extraordinary faith. And so we refer to this section of the Bible as the "Hall of Faith." Some of the Hall of Faith inductees include:

> Abel, Abraham, Isaac, Noah, Sarah, Moses, Gideon, Barak, David, Jephthah, Samuel and yes, even Rahab the harlot (prostitute).

Several of the individuals named above were revered because of their faithfulness. Many lived before Calvary's Cross and were excluded from receiving the promises available to us; still they championed the cause of faithfulness. They came from all walks of life and were challenged in different ways to exemplify faith. Some were miraculously delivered, some even died as martyrs, while maintaining their faith in God. But the one thing that unites this distinguished panel of honorees is that they had Faith in the promises of God.

Faith to Obtain God's Promises

The faith of Noah enabled him to prepare for a flood although it had never rained before on the face of the earth. Noah's response to his faith in God was to construct an ark, during which his faith was tested.

How was his faith tested?

> *"And every plant of the field before it was in the earth, and every herb of the field before it grew: for the LORD God had not caused it to rain upon the earth, and there was not a man to till the ground."* (Gen. 2:5).

Noah's faith was tested almost immediately. According to the scripture above, it had never rained on the face of the earth. Isn't God awesome? He plants vegetation but has no mechanism for watering it. We know this because the scripture specifically states, it had never rain before, yet the vegetation flourishes. Once again, God-gebra is in full effect by performing the impossible right in front of our eyes.

So now God tells Noah to build an ark and as we mentioned above, Noah had never seen rain. Has God ever challenged you to take on a task or project that seems ludicrous in your eyes because of the circumstances? This scenario comparably speaking would be like God telling you to purchase a fur coat and build an igloo in Hawaii because He's going to send snow. And if that isn't enough so-called foolishness, imagine that you have never seen snow before in your life. I can imagine Noah's friends as he gathered the wood to construct the ark come by and say, "Noah you must be hallucinating because the weather forecast calls for sunny weather for the remainder of our lives, because it's never rained and right now its 85 degrees and sunny, not a cloud in the sky."

One thing's for certain, if God speaks it, it's surely coming to pass no matter how long it takes or how ridiculous it might look. Sure enough, after celebrating his 600th birthday, Noah witnessed rain for the first time and unfortunately his friends were all "rained out". Noah and his family were saved from certain death because of his faith in the promises of God.

A Tested Faith

Scientists routinely have a process whereby they test portions of matter under certain circumstances, amidst various conditions, to see if their predicted outcome will result. Many devote much of their lives to testing a hypothesis to see if it will become a theory. Then they test that theory to see if a conclusive result occurs often and accurate enough to be deemed and thus labeled a law.

Just as an experiment seeks to prove a predicted outcome, likewise, every faith has to be tested. The moment you decide to serve God and commit your life to Him, the enemy is notified and decides to come after your faith.

I can recall one specific time when my faith was put on trial.

You are probably asking yourself, "How can someone's faith be placed on trial?" James 1:3 says, *"Knowing this, that the trying of your faith worketh patience…"* Believe me, if you keep walking with God, your faith can and will be put on trial. The question is not if, but when. And the bigger question is whether the verdict comes back from God with a judgment rendering you having been found pleasing in His sight because of your faith.

During the summer of 2004 my wife and I had been contemplating purchasing our second home as we noticed that our neighborhood and property value was starting to decline. We lived in this area for about eight years and felt like we should start petitioning God for the next place He would have us to live. So typically on the weekends, like many couples, we would attend open houses and walk through to get a feel of the type of floor plan that would accommodate our growing family. On this particular day, we visited Canton, Michigan which is a suburb roughly 20 minutes outside of Detroit. We had visited this area before because we have friends who live in Canton. Periodically, we had been invited to fellowships and as a result, we fell in love with the area. Everything looked fresh and new.

Well, we drove into this one particular subdivision and we noticed that all the homes looked different and weren't the typical "cookie cutter" style homes where they all looked alike. And upon further investigation, we noticed that these homes were not owned by one particular developer but several developers had purchased this land in order to build custom homes. Did I mention that these houses were simply beautiful? It seemed that the longer we were in this neighborhood, the more it felt like home. Still, in my mind, I knew I probably couldn't afford this area.

So one thing led to another and we agreed to at least call one of the builders to see what the process was to purchase one of these beautiful homes. My wife and I called three builders, but ironically only one builder called us back. The builder's name was Paul and he was the owner of a well known construction company in the area. Paul scheduled an appointment with us and invited us to see his product first-hand as he was in the process of finishing one of those beautiful custom homes. So my wife and I went to meet Paul and needless to say we were in awe at the quality and workmanship that he placed in his homes. We told Paul, we would think about it and get back to him. To this point, I still didn't know what Paul's prices were. We told Paul that we liked the custom home he had just finished and expressed to him that the square footage and other amenities were exactly what we would be interested in.

About a week later, Paul called to say that there were only a few lots available and that he was getting a great deal of inquiries from potential buyers, but he wanted us to have first pick of the existing lots. I remember my wife and I had decided to go on a fast and we agreed to fleece the Lord to see if this was His will based upon the builder's willingness to work within our very, very limited budget.

Saturday morning the phone rang, it was Paul. My wife gave me the phone and I remember Paul asking, "Mr. Blacksmith, what have you decided to do?" I said, "Paul I have a question for you. How much would it cost for us to custom build a house similar to the one you showed us recently?" Paul replied, "Houses in this subdivision start at about half a million and go all the way up, just shy of a million dollars." He went on to explain how we would have to first obtain a construction loan to purchase the land and once the house was completed the loan would be rolled into one mortgage. At this point I was thinking to myself, "Thanks for calling Paul, have a great day." Paul further explained, if this was something that we decided to do, he said he required at least $60,000 dollars down just to get the ball rolling. I distinctly recollect looking at my wife as if to say, "This can't be God because I don't have $60,000 to give Paul, in addition to securing a construction loan for the $100,000 dollar land purchase."

Feeling as if I had nothing to lose, I asked Paul one final question. I asked him if he would be willing to consider taking a $10,000 deposit to build the home instead of his lofty $60,000 retainer. Paul laughed sarcastically and said, "No Reputable Builder is going to honor these terms because of the exorbitant costs associated with building a custom home." Paul further contested that he would be liable to the bank if he built this home and for some unforeseen reason we reneged on the deal. Paul unexpectedly seemed agitated and offended. It was almost as if he felt that we were deliberately trying to question his credibility and devalue his craftsmanship. Not knowing what to say next, I was quiet and waited for Paul to make the next move. Paul hesitated and then responded by reiterating, "No builder would build a half million dollar house for a deposit of $10,000." I kindly agreed and told him that I felt his product was worth the $60,000 deposit or perhaps even more, but unfortunately, this was the best I could muster, considering my budget. All of a sudden, it was as if God Himself began to speak thru Paul.

Paul said, "Mr. Blacksmith, I absolutely can't do $10,000 as a deposit, but I can do $15,000." Wow, only $5,000 more. I thought to myself (Praise God!)—$5,000 is no where near the $60,000 as originally requested. Paul not only agreed to accept $15,000 as a retainer to build our home but he said he would be willing to accept the $15,000 deposit in $5,000 dollar increments throughout the building process. And if that wasn't enough concessions, Paul brought us to our knees with his next voluntary act. Listen to this… Paul agreed to also pay for our land out of his own pocket so we didn't have to secure a construction loan after all. Hallelujah!!! After making these allowances, Paul went on to compliment my wife and I by saying that when he first met us, he detected that there was something different about us. He said he wanted nothing less than to see our dream come to fruition (Glory to God!).

God showed up for us throughout this entire building process. There were several times when I didn't know where the next $5,000 dollar incremental payment was coming from. But God would just show up and I would get unexpected increases. I remember one specific time during the 2004 Christmas holiday, Paul called. He said, "I have some good news and some bad news." He said, "The bad news is that we made a mistake with the drawings of your house. The architect miscalculated your square footage and we mistakenly enlarged your home 100 square feet larger than originally planned—but the good news is…we are going to pay for it-Merry Christmas." This architectural miscalculation represented about a $15,000 dollar blessing!

Now as I mentioned earlier, anytime you decide to step out on faith and believe God, the devil is going to attack your faith. Consider Nehemiah: *"Now it came to pass, when Sanbal'lat, and Tobi'ah, and Geshem the Arabian, and the rest of our enemies, heard that I had builded the wall, and that there was no breach left therein; (though at that time I had not set up the doors upon the gates;) that Sanbal'lat and Geshem sent unto me, saying, Come, let us meet together in some one of the villages in the plain of Ono. But they thought to do me mischief. And I sent messengers unto them, saying, I am doing a great work, so that I cannot come down: why should the work cease, whilst I leave it, and come down to you?"* (Neh. 6:1-3). Like Nehemiah, whenever you attempt to do a great work, the enemy is going to try to "frustrate your purpose" and hinder the work of your hands by sowing seeds of doubt and discouragement.

Everything seemed to be going along smoothly. Paul was happy. We were happy. We had just completed the final walkthrough in November of 2005 and after eighteen months, we were finally ready to receive the promise and cross over into the land of Canaan. Everything seemed to be in place. We were told we had been approved for the mortgage; the builder received the certificate of occupancy indicating he passed the appropriate housing inspections and the closing date had been scheduled.

Then, from out of know where, we got a call from our mortgage broker who told us that the program we were supposedly pre-qualified for had now fallen thru. I thought to myself, "You gotta be kidding me!" Apparently, the lender refused to finalize the approval of the loan (we were already told we qualified for) with only days left before the closing date because of some minor insignificant technicality. The devil is a liar! It was as if someone pulled the rug out from under us. We went from the mountaintop to the valley in a matter of hours. I could feel my mind shifting from praise to discouragement. I even began to question God and ask, "If the *blessings of the Lord maketh rich and addeth no sorrow* (Prov. 10:22), why do I have tears in my eyes instead of a smile on my face? Why would you dangle something in front of my face and not give me the desire of my heart?"

To make matters worse, I had recently finalized a lease agreement for my previous home, and therefore, was contractually obligated to move out. And, considering I exercised this lease agreement with my new tenant, who just so happens to be an attorney, I didn't feel compelled to breach the contract (I am sure you understand why). So now I can't move into my new home because I don't have financing and I can't return to my previous home because it's been leased out. Also keep in mind, if I don't close the loan within a certain period after the house has been completed, I become liable to pay the builder a financial penalty of $1500 per day until the loan is closed. And lastly, my integrity as a Christian is on the line. Remember, Paul decided to bless us by doing in his estimation what "No reputable builder would do" by building a custom home out of his own pocket. I felt totally devastated. I didn't know what Paul's religious beliefs were but I wanted him to see God's Glory throughout this entire process, and now this was in jeopardy. As it stood, I was caught between a rock and a hard place.

It's Yours, but You've Got to Take It!

I can remember my Pastor asking me to lead corporate prayer not knowing that I was feeling like God had forsaken me. I distinctly recall the exhortation God had given me for that evening's prayer focus. It was entitled, "It's already yours, but you've got to take it!" During this exhortation, I chronicled the account of Moses commissioning twelve men to spy out the land that God had promised Israel as an inheritance.

> *"And Caleb stilled the people before Moses, and said, let us go up at once, and possess it; for we are well able to overcome it. But the men who went up with him said, we be not able to go up against the people; for they are Stronger than we. And there we saw the giants, the sons of Anak, which come of the giants: and we were in our own sight as grasshoppers, and so we were in their sight"* (Num. 13:30-33).

After the twelve men returned with their scouting report, only two men, Joshua and Caleb had enough faith to believe that victory was eminent and assured. The ten others report their findings and convinced Moses that according to their faith, it was impossible to defeat the inhabitants and stake claim to what God had already pre-destined as their inheritance.

Because these ten men lacked faith, the Bible tells us in Numbers 14:36, the ten scouts who had incited rebellion against the Lord by spreading discouraging reports about the land were struck dead with a plague. Of the twelve that were originally deployed, only Joshua and Caleb remained alive.

I went on to share with the people of God that your faith will determine what you can have in life and when you can have it. Let me explain further. Several decades later in the Book of Joshua, Rahab explains to Joshua's spies that during Moses administration we knew the Lord had given you this land. Rahab testifies,

"For we have heard how the Lord hath given you the land, and that your terror is fallen upon us, and that all the inhabitants of the land faint because of you. For we have heard how the Lord has dried up the Red Sea for you, when you came out of Egypt; and what ye did unto the two kings of the Amorites that were on the other side Jordan. And as soon as we heard these things, our hearts did melt, neither did there remain any more courage in any man, because of you: for the Lord your

God, he is God in heaven above, and in earth beneath" (Josh. 2:10-11).

To paraphrase Rahab, "We have been living on land that we knew the Israelites owned because of your God. As a matter of fact, we had our bags packed and we were waiting in fear for Israel to come and evict us, but we stayed because no one ever showed up. Even being as big and intimidating as the ten faithless spies said we looked; we were even the more terrified of you because of the magnanimity of your God. The land was always yours, but no one came to take it."

As I concluded prayer that evening, my Pastor asked my wife and me to stay after service because he wanted to talk to us. Surprisingly he had tape recorded the exhortation and demanded that we sit and hear it ourselves. After listening he gave a CD of the message and told us to believe our own words and that God was getting ready to show Himself mightily because of our faith.

Faith to Deliver

My wife and I continued fighting the good fight of faith and the following week we got a call from our mortgage broker saying that she had received an update from the lender. The lender indicated that we could not qualify for the original program but there was another program that we qualified for (Hallelujah!). We agreed to participate in this new program as we believed this to be the will of God.

On December 28, 2005 at roughly 11 o' clock in the morning, my wife and I received the keys to our brand new home. After eighteen months and countless hours of fasting and praying, we stood in the parking lot after the closing and just praised God for all that we had endured. We experienced spiritual warfare of monumental proportions, why? Because we chose to believe God for what others said could never happen. This was one of the happiest days of our lives.

It was December 31, 2005 when we finally moved into our new home. God really did save the best for last. Our close friends stopped by and we christened our new home with prayer and praise until it was time for us to prepare for "watch night" service to usher in the New Year. We were both excited and exhausted, but nonetheless, committed to attending church in order to praise God for all He had done.

Ironically, when we arrived at church, my pastor asked me if I would share my testimony. After giving my testimony, he spoke these words that I will never forget. He shouted, "Persecution always Precedes Promotion." Amen! I replied. As I started walking back to my seat, my pastor interrupted me and said, "Since this is the last day of 2005 and God has promoted you naturally with a new home, God also wants to promote you spiritually, so from now on, you won't be known as just Minister Ivan, but you will be recognized as Elder Ivan Blacksmith!" I was overwhelmed and immediately fell to my knees and wept at the awesomeness of God.

Only God could recompense my family for all we had been through and turn what seemed to be unfruitful and unproductive into a positive result by allowing us to not only go into the year 2006 with a new home but more importantly, God saw fit to elevate our servant hood in the process.

Brothers and Sisters this journey was never about materialistic gain or building a house of brick and mortar. It was always about the ability to believe the promises of God in the face of severe adversity by enduring the "testing of our faith period," which sets the tone for God-gebra to be activated.

The Fear Factor

The arch enemy to faith is fear. Fear can be best described as **F**alse **E**vidence **A**ppearing **R**eal which actually spells **FEAR**. Notice the definition implies false and appearing. These words identify strategies that the enemy uses to suffocate our faith. By implementing fear, he can distort our faith by altering the perspective of our reality. Let me explain. There are three characteristics of faith.

1. Faith must have a valid ***content*** (Gen. 17:5).
    —The content of Abraham's faith was revelation of God.
2. Faith must have a valid ***object*** (Gen. 17:5-6).
    —The object of Abraham's faith was God, giver of revelation.

3. Faith must have a valid ***purpose*** (Gen. 12:1-3).

—Purpose of Abraham's faith was to become father of many nations.

If the enemy can manipulate any one of these three characteristics, he can control us like a puppeteer. Since the enemy cannot destroy the promises of God, he employs fear as a tactic to attack our faith and keep us frustrated and doubtful of obtaining the promises of God. In either case, if we give up, the blessing is forfeited.

Three Ways the Enemy Attacks Our Faith

1. Fear & Deception: commonly used to conceal and protect the enemy and his advances, to hide his real purposes. A confused faithless people will rarely achieve victory.

Moses & the Children of Israel

> *"And it came to pass, when Pharaoh had let the people go, that God led them not through the way of the land of the Philistines, although that was near; for God said, Lest peradventure the people repent when they see war, and they return to Egypt"* (Ex. 13: 17-18).

> *"And when Pharaoh drew nigh, the children of Israel lifted up their eyes, and, behold, the Egyptians marched after them; and*

> *they were sore afraid: and the children of Israel cried out unto the Lord. And they said unto Moses, Because there were no graves in Egypt, hast thou taken us away to die in the wilderness? wherefore hast thou dealt thus with us, to carry us forth out of Egypt? Is not this the word that we did tell thee in Egypt, saying, Let us alone, that we may serve the Egyptians? For it had been better for us to serve the Egyptians, than that we should die in the wilderness"* (Ex. 14:10-14).

The devil's deception injected so much fear in the children of Israel that it rendered them paralyzed to believe and obey God's Word. But Moses shook them out of their fearful paralysis by declaring, *"Fear ye not, stand still, and see the salvation of the LORD, which he will show to you today: for the Egyptians whom ye have seen today, ye shall see them again no more for ever"* (Ex. 14:13).

How many times has fear and deception caused you to abort (give up prematurely) your seed or blessing (an idea, a business, or deliverance) that God has promised to birth in your spirit? God expects for us to water and nurture this seed with faith by trusting He will provide the increase (1 Cor. 3:6). Whenever God impregnates us with purpose, the enemy's job is to come along and inject us with fear which acts as a type of "morning after pill" that prevents our seed (plan of God) from developing. So when we become hesitant or reluctant to "carry full term" because of fear, we commit "spiritual abortion." Fear and deception work hand in hand—each standing on the opposite end of faith, attempting to crush it like a vice grip. By allowing faith to provide the proper prenatal care we increase our chances of having a natural birth (no complications) filled with the joy and excitement of giving birth to a miracle.

The devil is a master of deception: don't let him fool your faith.

2. Intimidation: used to defeat an enemy without physical confrontation usually by threats and the appearance of overwhelming strength. A fearful and discouraged people have already been defeated.

David & Goliath

> *"Now the Philistines gathered together their armies to battle, and were gathered together at Shochoh, which belongeth to Judah, and pitched between Shochoh and Aze'kah, in Ephes— dam'mim. And Saul and the men of Israel were gathered together, and pitched by the valley of Elah, and set the battle in array against the Philistines. And the Philistines stood on a mountain on the one side, and Israel stood on a mountain on the other side: and there was a valley between them"* (1 Sam. 17:1-3).

Here we have the Children of Israel on one side of the mountain and their enemy on the other side with only a valley between them.

"And there went out a champion out of the camp of the Philistines, named Goli'ath, of Gath, whose height was six cubits and a span. And he had a helmet of brass upon his head, and he was armed with a coat of mail; and the weight of the coat was five thousand shekels of brass. And he had greaves of brass upon his legs, and a target of brass between his shoulders. And the staff of his spear was like a weaver's beam; and his spear's head weighed six hundred shekels of iron: and one bearing a shield went before him. And he stood and cried unto the armies of Israel, and said unto them, why are ye come out to set your battle in array? am not I a Philistine, and ye servants to Saul? Choose you a man for you, and let him come down to me. If he be able to fight with me, and to kill me, then will we be your servants: but if I prevail against him, and kill him, then shall ye be our servants, and serve us. And the Philistine said, I defy the armies of Israel this day; give me a man, that we may fight together. When Saul and all Israel heard those words of the Philistine, they were dismayed, and greatly afraid" (1 Sam. 17:4-11).

So the Philistine champion openly challenged any soldier of Israel to a fight to the death. The Bible let's us know that Israel's army was greatly afraid. Why are they so afraid? They were afraid because of what they saw. Remember the definition. The enemy uses intimidation to defeat and opponent without physical confrontation, usually with the appearance of overwhelming strength. The enemy is masterful at creating an illusion of strength in order to deactivate the faith of a Christian which now renders him vulnerable to his attacks.

Notice the size of Goliath. He was almost 10 feet tall. Notice his uniform. He wore a helmet of brass and a coat of mail with brass on his legs and a weaver's beam that weighed over 50 pounds. Everything used to describe Goliath's stature and battle array provoked the sense of sight and was portrayed as "excessively big." This diabolical strategy was by design in order to shatter the faith of the Israelites by instilling fear. Think about it. What could Goliath actually hit with a spear that size? The laws of physics suggest that the spear could not have been very accurate because it was top heavy. If Goliath had thrown the spear, according to the laws of aerodynamics, it would have just toppled over, similar to throwing a large sledge hammer. The hammer's weight is centered in one spot which reduces its aerodynamic precision as a projectile because of its design. This spear was nothing more than a "menacing looking" awe inspiring weapon of futile inadequacy. So in other words, Goliath never meant to ever throw the spear, the same way he never expected to fight. He made his living "selling woof tickets" and relying on the tactics of intimidation to win his battles. Goliath's aim and intention was to scare the people of God into submission.

How many times do we allow the devil to intimidate us with "circumstantial Goliath's"? It takes a small ruddy shepherd boy, which no one considers significant, to come along and show us what a faith-filled, battle ready warrior can do when armed with the anointing of God. The power of faith will always expose the giants in your life for what they really are, opportunities for victory. And in doing so, we learn to see challenges of faith as mere passageways for continuous maturation in God.

3. Propaganda: lies to enemy troops (Christians) in an attempt to simulate troop movement. This tactic can stymie the enemy and in doing so, stimulate them to act outside of their normal pattern of behavior, all the while drawing them away from safety.

Adam & Eve

> *"And the LORD God took the man, and put him into the Garden of Eden to dress it and to keep it. And the LORD God commanded the man, saying, of every tree of the garden thou mayest freely eat: but of the tree of the knowledge of good and evil, thou shalt not eat of it: for in the day that thou eatest thereof thou shalt surely die"* (Gen. 2:17).

This is a very familiar account in the Book of Genesis whereby God is setting the ground rules for Adam and Eve regarding his expectations of their existence. He gives them free reign of the Garden of Eden and extends to them every courtesy imaginable, except of course, allowing eating from "the tree of knowledge of good and evil."

> *"Now the serpent was more subtile than any beast of the field which the LORD God had made. And he said unto the*

woman, Yea, hath God said, Ye shall not eat of every tree of the garden? And the woman said unto the serpent, We may eat of the fruit of the trees of the garden: but of the fruit of the tree which is in the midst of the garden, God hath said, Ye shall not eat of it, neither shall ye touch it, lest ye die. And the serpent said unto the woman, Ye shall not surely die: for God doth know that in the day ye eat thereof, then your eyes shall be opened, and ye shall be as gods, knowing good and evil" (Gen. 3:1-4).

These scriptures provide a textbook lesson on believing God's truth instead of the devil's lies. Interestingly, the Bible forewarns us about the devil's mastery of tongue by being able to talk out of both sides of his mouth. According to the scriptures, he was more subtle than any other beast of the field. So immediately this scripture should have pre-warned Adam and Eve to the craftiness of the serpent. However, the serpent appeals cunningly to our desire to be superior to God. How, you might say? Notice what the serpent says after God establishes His ordinance. God speaks profoundly and declares, *"for in the day that thou eat of the fruit thou shall surely die."* Now the serpent, obviously having heard this decree, comes behind God and debunks His rule by stating the following, *"you shall not surely die."*

This narrative represents many scenarios in life where we are going to be challenged to believe God's Word as absolute truth or suffer the consequences of embracing a lie. The Bible refers to the devil as the father of lies (John 8:44).

Many of us have fallen prey to "The Devil's Lies" which have said:

- You will never be anything in life.
- You will never get over that abusive relationship.
- You will never get married.
- Your ministry is not of God.
- You can't raise your children alone.
- You will never get off of drugs.
- You will never get over depression.
- You will never get out of debt.
- You will never be forgiven by God.
- You will be nothing in life but a gangster.
- Your business will never be a success.

Conversely, God cannot lie (Titus 1:2).

We should believe "The Truth" in which God says:

- I can do all things through Him.
- I am more than a conqueror.
- I can have eternal life.
- I shall have good success.
- I can live abundantly.
- I am from a royal priesthood.
- If my parents forsake me, He will raise me up.
- He will never leave or forsake me.
- He will open up the windows of heaven to bless me.

- He will keep my mind in perfect peace.
- He will make my enemies my footstool.

These are the encouraging truths that should be entrenched in our spirits. So whose report will you believe? We are commanded to believe God's truth as opposed to the lies of the enemy. This should be easy, considering His very existence is molded in truth and therefore makes it impossible for Him to be a liar. This being the case, why are we more apt to believe a lie when faced with a series of challenging circumstances? Here's why.

The serpent does something very divisive after he contends that Adam & Eve will not surely die. He infers that God is afraid to reveal some level of truth to them for fear they (Adam & Eve) will be His equal. Look at what he says. *"For God doth know that in the day ye eat thereof, then your eyes shall be opened, and ye shall be as gods, knowing good and evil."* Upon further investigation, we see that word "as" gods which means, likeness to but not the definite article. The devil is up to his tricks again by trying to forge and bend the truth. As Christians, if we are not careful, we can fall prey to his half truths—and a half truth is a whole lie.

The devil's modus operandi has always been to imitate the likeness of God. He is the "spiritual knockoff" of an original God. The Bible warns us of his manipulations and illusions by saying, *"Be sober, be vigilant; because your adversary the devil, as a roaring lion, walketh about, seeking whom he may devour"* (1 Pet. 5:8). As a master of deception and disguise, the devil's intent is for us to pay a higher cost for a cheaper living. In other words, the devil wants us to pay "Ritz Carlton" hotel prices but live beneath our God-given privileges at the Motel 6. He wants us to choose his lies instead of the abundant living found in the truth of God's Word.

This is a revelation many of us need to understand because the enemy is constantly thinking like a chess player, usually five moves ahead of his current position. He would have us to believe that we should possess or covet something that God knows is not healthy for us and in our haste to possess it, it devours our souls. Always bear in mind; you don't have to live a lie, when Jesus died for you to have the truth.

Chapter 5
The Value of (X)

As we prepare to discuss the fourth and final component of the God-gebra equation, a quick repeat reminds us that the first coefficient a, stands for An Impossibility. The second coefficient b, is described as Beyond Hope. The third coefficient c, represents a Certain Measure of Faith. For the last entity of the God-gebra concept (a+b+c=x), we will look at the importance of The Value of "X."

The letter X is the 24th letter in the alphabet and depending upon how it is positioned, can be interpreted in a variety of ways by our society. Let's identify some of these ways.

The letter "X" can be associated with owning the video blockbuster known as "Xbox", or using Microsoft's "XP" operating system. Other descriptions include the X chromosome which is linked to determining the sex of child. Advertisers use the phrase "Brand X" to describe a competing brand or product which, while not named, is implied to be of inferior quality. Many people often recognize X as the first letter for the common abbreviation of the word Christmas. Then there's X-rays. These are a type of electromagnetic radiation, widely used by doctors for diagnostic purposes. In Roman numerals, X denotes the number 10; with a horizontal line drawn above it, it means 10,000. Even our clothing sizes are noted as using the letter X which stands for extra (XS, XL, XXL). People have also taken on the letter X as part of their name. Malcolm X: The African-American activist Malcolm Little changed his surname to X in 1952 to signify that his original name had been lost in slavery. X has also been connected to finding the elusive pirate's treasure. From this treasure hunt we have coined the phrase "X marks the spot". And lastly, the letter X has been manipulated by humanity to symbolize its most spiritually degrading meaning to date. The letter X has been amplified to the third power to form "XXX"—what our culture has affectionately labeled as Adult Material or Pornography. So as we have evidenced, the value of "X" in our society varies depending upon who's using it and how it's being utilized.

For the purposes of God-gebra, I want to focus on the value of X relative to a mathematical symbol for an unknown variable or quantity. Upon further investigation of the laws of algebra, we find that most times when attempting to solve an equation you are not given the value of X. Instead, you are to apply the rules of algebra by using a series of mathematical calculations. The challenge is to incorporate the known values into the equation in order to reveal the value of X.

Paradoxically, God-gebra works in much the same fashion. How? Many times in life we are not given all the resources (variables) we feel are necessary in order to accomplish (solve) or attain certain goals. God in His infinite wisdom purposely does not always connect all the dots as to allow us to see His hand (the value of X) in our situation. Scripture validates this by stating, *"For my thoughts are not your thoughts, neither are your ways my ways, saith the LORD. For as the heavens are higher than the earth, so are my ways higher than your ways, and my thoughts than your thoughts"* (Isaiah 55:7-8). In doing so, God appears to be withholding what we consider necessities, only to allow us to flourish even more with less. This is the priceless value of X. No matter how bad your childhood, marriage, job, drug addiction, family or past failures may have been, the value of X can still solve life's equations without the benefit of having what others consider to be "known variables" or all the "I's dotted and T's crossed".

Perhaps you come from a single parent home, were raised on the other side of the tracks, addicted to drugs, had a child out of wedlock, or even spent some time in jail. The value of X will balance these lop-sided equations and allow what you didn't have to still work out for the good.

Generation "X"

The traditional definition of the Generation X is marked by a lack of optimism. Overwhelming skepticism, alienation and a gross mistrust in traditional values flourish in combination with a negative attitude regarding a positive outlook for the future. According to many sociology professors, this approach to reality stems from the fact that they have fewer positive role models and are presented with limited solutions for limitless world problems. As a result, many fear they will be forced to inherit a state of affairs unlike any generation which preceded them.

The media portrays this culture as a group of saggy pants, backwards baseball cap wearing, underachieving slackers with multiple earrings, sporting body piercings who seem more concerned about "Bling Bling" than being their brothers keeper. I believe this behavior is a reflection of what they are missing. Let me explain.

Our current generation is reacting to what they are lacking. This rebellious spirit is the residue of a world that has strayed further and further away from spiritual fulfillment and only God has the spiritual tonic to revive this ailing world. The scripture reveals, *"If my people, which are called by my name, shall humble themselves, and pray, and seek my face, and turn from their wicked ways; then will I hear from heaven, and will forgive their sin, and will heal their land"* (2 Chron. 7:14).

We need God to heal our land and here's one example why. All across this country children live in single family homes simply because their father was more content to live out his "Don Juan" fantasy lifestyle of fornication and sin rather than channeling his efforts into being the father that God intended. Men have grown content with making only a biological contribution but failing to establish a spiritual covering.

This is the type of scenario in which Godgebra specializes; when something is missing or lacking. In this scenario, the Value of X is a missing father. God-gebra will provide you the benefits of fatherhood without having a natural father.

A Father to the Fatherless

"When my father and my mother forsake me, then the LORD will take me up" (Psalm 27:10).

While studying and researching this scripture, I found that many experts have considered the possibility that this verse could have been written by someone other than David. Why you might ask? The reason this possibility is considered is because scripturally we can't find where David is forsaken by his parents. As I thought and prayed about this spiritual quagmire, I considered another possibility to what David's intention might have been. The scripture starts off "when."

The word "when" translated means, "in the event of time and place." In other words, this scripture is declaring that "in the event my father or mother forsake me, then the Lord will take me up." This means, "If my father walks out or if my mother puts me up for adoption." I believe God was giving David and many of us a contingency clause. He wanted us to know that whatever happens, He is our Jehovah Jireh and will provide for our needs. He will still cause us to triumph without being the benefactor of a natural father.

How does a person who has never had a father learn to become a father? God-gebra! Normally you experience learning from observing a pattern or a blue print. In other words, it's no surprise that you learn to become a father when you experienced someone being a father to you.

Here is how the value of X worked in my life.

I was born an only child to Frank and Mary Blacksmith. Shortly after I was born, my father chose to take his resentment toward my mother out on me by not playing an active role in my life. He wanted no part in my rearing and development as a child. It was as if he purchased a trendy sweater and decided to return it because he had a change of heart.

Imagine the aggression, hurt and embarrassment I endured while growing up. I can remember when parent teacher's conferences and other forms of parental involvement came around. Someone would always seem to ask the million dollar question, where is your father? Little did they know, I had asked myself that same question hundreds of times before.

My Father

My father was a very successful entrepreneur. I used to dream of working along side of him at our family's business. I often imagined him standing at the finish line as I placed first during one of my high school track meets. I dreamed of seeing his smile as I was recognized for my academic achievements during my collegiate commencements. I envisioned him handing over the keys to the family business and hearing him say, "Son, I am well pleased in your accomplishments thus far, but my prayer is that you will take what God has blessed me to accomplish to the next level and one day challenge your son to carry on the same way that I am challenging you." Then, as if I had hit a brick wall, the glaring reality of being without a father settled in once more.

Even after my father moved out, my mother would always acknowledge God as our True Provider. "It's not your father's resources but God who will make the crooked path straight," she would say. "Don't worry about an inheritance, God has an inheritance that will pay eternal dividends." God seemed to give my mother an extra anointing because instead of telling me about how no-good my natural father was, and slandering his name, she told me about a spiritual Father who would never leave me nor forsake me (Heb 13:5).

Three ways God taught me fatherhood:

1. God used my mother to teach me Biblical discipline.
2. My mother represented a Godly example.
3. God filled me with The Holy Ghost (Act 2:38)

These three lessons taught me the meaning of respecting others while respecting myself. I could hold my head up although I was fatherless, because God gave me my identity and not the thugs on the street. (Mothers, who may be reading this book, don't discount the example you live before your children everyday. They are watching to see godliness in your life).

As I reflect over my life, it still causes me to tear up because I miss what "could have been" and in actuality, "should have been"—a beautiful harmonious relationship between a father and his beloved son. There's an old saying, *"Experience is your hardest teacher because you take the test before you learn the lesson."* I can say that even though those tests were difficult, God has been the Father that has tutored me through life's lessons. Today, God has taught me using the Value of X (being fatherless) how to be a God-fearing parent to my two beautiful children. Ironically, I learned how to be something to my children that my father wasn't to me.

Let's be real. It can be quite painful growing up fatherless or motherless because the enemy will try to plant seeds in your mind to depreciate your value and lower your self esteem. The statistics have even doubted your ability to persevere and on many occasions, have referred to you as coming from a broken home. But the statisticians didn't take into account during their preliminary analysis the spiritual significance of God-gebra. Hallelujah! The value of X declares that a broken home is not a home without a mother or father. A broken home is a home without God.

"X" Convict

Incarceration is generally perceived as very depressing, and only society's worst and wayward are given memberships at our country's correctional facilities. After completing their debt to society, usually defined by time served, the prisoner is forgiven of past discretions and re-introduced back into the society in which they once wreaked havoc. The prisoner is now considered an "Ex-convict".

Conversely, the Bible speaks of such a day of adjudication by declaring, *"Therefore if any man be in Christ, he is a new creature: old things are passed away; behold, all things are become new"* (2 Cor. 5:17).

Just as an Ex-convict is forgiven of past discretions once their debt to society has been paid in full, likewise in the realm of God, when an individual fulfills the complete list of salvation requirements according to Acts 2:38, God totally forgives his/her previous sins. Never to be reminded of past transgressions for an eternity—now that's what I call true forgiveness!

Forgiveness is a powerful device. Some of us have no problem believing God has forgiven us, but because of past failures, we find it difficult and in some cases impossible to forgive ourselves. The Bible refutes this notion by stating, *"If the Son therefore shall make you free, ye shall be free indeed"* (John 8:36).

Because sin does not vary in degree, no sin is better or worse than another (Rev. 21:8). This is a trick of the enemy designed to keep you bound in self pity while taking the focus off of the power of Jesus Christ to forgive sins. *"But if we walk in the light, as he is in the light, we have fellowship one with another, and the blood of Jesus Christ his Son cleanseth us from all sin"* (1 John 1:7).

I am reminded of the time when Jesus healed the man sick of the palsy. *"And, behold, they brought to Him a man sick of the palsy, lying on a bed: and Jesus seeing their faith said unto the sick of the palsy; Son, be of good cheer; thy sins be forgiven thee. And, behold, certain of the scribes said within themselves, This man blasphemeth. And Jesus knowing their thoughts said, Wherefore think ye evil in your hearts? For whether is easier, to say, Thy sins be forgiven thee; or to say, Arise, and walk? But that ye may know that the Son of man hath power on earth to forgive sins, (then saith He to the sick of the palsy,) Arise, take up thy bed, and go unto thine house. And he arose, and departed to his house. But when the multitudes saw it, they marvelled, and glorified God, which had given such power unto men"* (Matt. 9:2-8).

What power does this scripture suggest that we have been given? We have been given the power to forgive ourselves and others. If Jesus gave us this power, why do we allow the enemy to manipulate our minds by preventing us from forgiving others? When we forgive others, we release their shackles and in the process, free ourselves. Jesus continues teaching the scribes a Bible class on forgiveness.

Let us further study the miracle of the palsied man. The scribes neglected to believe that Jesus could forgive sin. In order to demonstrate that He had power to forgive sins, He healed the palsied man. This miracle was wrought for the express purpose of illustrating the importance of forgiving sin, and demonstrating its power. Jesus said to the palsied man, *"Arise, take up thy bed, and go unto thine house,"* that they, and ye, might know His power to forgive sin. For that reason, the power showcased in the healing of that man is the power bestowed in the forgiveness of sin. Jesus not only forgave this man but went one step further by healing him. Similarly, we are to forgive others and likewise, too will receive our healing.

God is so awesome! Only God-gebra can take a person that has never been forgiven and teach them forgiveness in order to demonstrate the importance of forgiving others. God-gebra further reveals that as we practice forgiveness, two individuals are released from their bands, the person whom you forgave and "you" for being willing to forgive. Don't be content to remain bound in the prison of un-forgiveness when God has already set you free!

The "X" Factor

The X-factor is a term used to describe the missing link for success of a certain object or systematic process. And in times past, because there has been a void of these heroics by the X-factor, failure became imminent. For example, until Michael Jordan joined the Chicago Bulls, they were a sub par underachieving basketball team. But with Michael Jordan they became perennial championship contenders and dominated the 1990's by winning an unprecedented 6 NBA Championships. Michael Jordan was indeed the X factor.

Similarly, the game of golf for many years was considered a country club sport to be enjoyed and dominated by wealthy white socialites. As a matter of fact, there were some golf courses that would deny access simply based on the color of your skin. Interest in the game of golf was so low at one point that television ratings suffered and the PGA (The Professional Golf Association) would consistently rank among the worst viewed sporting events when compared to their professional counterparts like football and baseball. Along comes Eldrick "Tiger" Woods a multi-racial phenom who has revolutionized the game of golf. Woods is credited with prompting a major surge of interest in the game of golf among minorities and young people in the United States. Tiger Woods' achievements to date rank him among the most successful golfers of all time. Currently the "world's number one player". Woods was the highest paid professional athlete in 2006, having earned an estimated $100 million from winnings and endorsements. In 2006, at the age of 30, he won his eleventh and twelfth professional major golf championship and has more wins on the PGA tour than any other active golfer. He is the only active golfer in the top 10 in career major wins and career PGA tour wins. Tiger Woods is undisputebly the X factor for the game of golf.

"Wherefore, as by one man sin entered into the world, and death by sin; and so death passed upon all men, for that all have sinned: (For until the law sin was in the world: but sin is not imputed when there is no law. Nevertheless death reigned from Adam to Moses, even over them that had not sinned after the similitude of Adam's transgression, who is the figure of him that was to come. But not as the offence, so also is the free gift. For if through the offence of one many be dead, much more the grace of God, and the gift by grace, which is by one man, Jesus Christ, hath abounded unto many. And not as it was by one

that sinned, so is the gift: for the judgment was by one to condemnation, but the free gift is of many offences unto justification. For if by one man's offence death reigned by one; much more they which receive abundance of grace and of the gift of righteousness shall reign in life by one, Jesus Christ). Therefore as by the offence of one judgment came upon all men to condemnation; even so by the righteousness of one the free gift came upon all men unto justification of life. For as by one man's disobedience many were made sinners, so by the obedience of one shall many be made righteous" (Rom. 5:12-19).

The abovementioned scriptures are crediting the obedience of Jesus Christ as being solely responsible for having made many righteous because of His redemptive blood shed for us on Calvary's Cross. In other words, Jesus is the ultimate X-factor.

The Situation

After the fall of man in the Garden of Eden, the deceiver (Satan) presented God with what he determined to be certain victory for the powers of darkness because of the impending impossible situation. The enemy felt there was no way he could lose. The scripture stated, *"For the wages of sin is death"* (Rom. 6:23). The enemy was successful through his trickery and craftiness to convince Adam and Eve to partake of the forbidden fruit. After

Adam and Eve partook of the fruit, the enemy knew that God would have to answer these charges with death, by virtue of the previous scripture. Something had to die! Nothing would give Satan more pleasure than to provoke God into killing the very creation He loved beyond compare. So God reviews the evidence and listens to the charges brought against Him by Satan, and in His infinite wisdom, begins concocting a plan. He ultimately concludes as Satan listens intently, that man's dilemma is sin. God thinks to Himself, "My Word does declare that no one is exempt from paying the penalty for sin which is death." I can imagine Satan sitting there salivating at the fact that God appears to be trapped in a "Catch 22" and will be forced to slaughter His most cherished creation. But little did Satan know that God had devised a predestinated solution for such a time as this.

The Plan

God-gebra completes its greatest work to date. With minimal deliberation, God decides to execute a fool proof plan for redemption. Since no one else is capable of doing what only God can, He decides that He will become a man (John 1:14) and die for our sins (John12:24).

To better understand why God selected this redemptive strategy, let's conduct a quick review of the Old Testament, which prepared people for the coming of Jesus Christ. Among the many events outlined in the Old Testament, the annual celebration of the Day of Atonement is among the greatest celebrated. Yom Kippur, according to the regulations of the Book of Leviticus, was the day when two healthy unblemished goats were chosen for the slaughter as they represented sinless perfection. The High Priest which acted as a mediator between the sinful stiff-necked people and the Holy Majestic God would take one goat and lay his hands on it while confessing the sins of the people. Following this confession, he would sacrifice (kill) this goat, which acted as a substitute for the sinners who rightly deserved a severe death because of their sinful ways.

The second goat, ironically called a scapegoat, would then be sent gallivanting into the wilderness in a direction considered away from the "sinners." This act symbolized the fact that the scapegoat had taken their sins far away. Only by completely understanding the role of these two goats can God's ultimate plan be appreciated. Think about it. There were two animals but only one was slaughtered for the propitiation of sin.

Now let's continue unveiling God's plan to redeem His people from their sin.

Much to Satan's dismay, God is never taken aback or caught off guard. Because of God-gebra, He always has a contingency plan and at some point during His formulation of eternity, He decides that Jesus Christ (God manifested in the flesh) would become the X-factor for mankind (following the Old Testament remedy for exterminating sin). Jesus Christ was sent from heaven to earth to fulfill a mission of saving mankind from the "guttermost to the uttermost" by eradicating sin once and for all.

By offering Himself as atonement for sin, He shut Satan's accusatory mouth by fulfilling the scripture which called for death as a result of Adam and Eve's transgression in order to "reconcile" man's debt of sin. Jesus Christ is without question the *"Lamb slain from the foundation of the world"* (Rev.13:8).

The Result

As the X-factor, Jesus came to give us what we were missing in order to live an abundant prosperous (sinless) life.

> *"The thief cometh not, but for to steal, and to kill, and to destroy: I am come that they might have life, and that they might have it more abundantly"* (John 10:10).

Jesus is the bridge between the world and eternity. His humility on Calvary should alleviate any ambiguity surrounding his mission and purpose for coming to earth.

> *"He made Himself of no reputation, taking the form of a bondservant, and coming in the likeness of men. And being found in appearance as a man, He humbled Himself and became obedient to the point of death, even the death of the cross"* (Phil. 2:6).

Speaking of the cross, Jesus realized that in order for us to re-unite with God the Father, He would have to suffer many atrocities. I am reminded of when Jesus went to Calvary and was hung between two thieves symbolizing the space between humanity and eternity.

> *"And when they were come to the place, which is called Calvary, there they crucified him, and the malefactors, one on the right hand, and the other on the left. And one of the malefactors which were hanged railed on him, saying, If thou be Christ, save thyself and us. But the other answering rebuked him, saying, Dost not thou fear God, seeing thou art in the same condemnation? And we indeed justly; for we receive the due reward of our deeds: but this man hath done nothing amiss. And he said unto Jesus, Lord, remember me when thou comest into thy kingdom. And Jesus said unto him, Verily I say unto thee, Today shalt thou be with me in paradise"* (Luke 23:33-43).

Of the two malefactors (thieves), only one recognized that Jesus Christ was the X-factor sent here on behalf of mankind. The other malefactor (thief) doubts Jesus' ability by sarcastically suggesting, *"save thyself and us."* The sorrowful malefactor admits his guilt and states for the record, we are guilty and justified to receive our punishment but declares that Jesus has done nothing wrong.

This limited conversation speaks volumes to us about the importance of confessing our sin and then repenting which means "completely turning away" from our previous deeds. Notice after the thief confesses and repents, Jesus immediately grants him a spiritual pardon just moments before His X-factor duties are completed. Jesus saves the dying thief by telling him, *"today thou shalt be with me in paradise."*

Complete "X"oneration

Why was the humble malefactor (thief) acquitted and exonerated of all charges? Were the malefactors guilty and deserving of death by crucifixion? The answer is yes! Then what caused Jesus to forgive one malefactor but not the other? Confession and Repentance! These two characteristics activated God-gebra and caused the X-factor (Jesus) to come alive in the midst of a dying situation. Confession and "true" Repentance will consistently stimulate Jesus Christ, through God's redemptive plan of salvation (Acts 2:38), to work on your behalf and grant you also a spiritual pardon instead of sentencing you to die in your sins (John 8:24).

> *"He then would have had to suffer often since the foundation of the world; but now, once at the end of the ages, He has appeared to put away sin by the sacrifice of Himself"* (Heb. 9:26).

X-treme Makeover

Extreme Makeover is a television program aired by "ABC" in which individuals volunteer to receive an extensive makeover in

Hollywood, California. The show depicts ordinary men and women undergoing "drastic physical alterations" involving plastic surgery, exercise regimens, hairdressing and wardrobing. Each episode begins with an individual's appearance depicted in usually the worst fashion and ends with the subjects' return to their families and friends, following their makeover, showing the reactions of their loved ones, who have not been allowed to see the incremental changes during the subjects' absence.

In a similar way, God-gebra will make use of the value of X to spiritually and naturally give us an X-treme makeover. God will make us a promise, which upon its fulfillment; will change our countenance and circumstances in a way where friends and family will fail to recognize us because of the X-treme makeover that God-gebra has performed. The story of Joseph is a classic example.

Joseph Received "An X-treme Makeover"

In the Book of Genesis, we find Joseph, the eleventh son of Jacob, whom God has favored. Joseph had dreams that he would be elevated above his brothers (Gen. 37:5-10). He saw himself standing with his eleven brothers around him bowing. These dreams confirmed the favor on Joseph's life and that God had planned to elevate Joseph according to this dream. But the next course of action did not correspond with the dreams. Because of his brother's hatred and jealousy towards him, Joseph was placed in a pit and ultimately sold into slavery. His journey down X-treme Makeover Boulevard continues with him being falsely accused, imprisoned and forgotten. In no way did these adversities line up with his dreams.

Eleven years had passed since Joseph was sold into Egypt, and yet the Divine promise conveyed in his dreams seemed farther than ever from fulfillment. But when God was through with it all, the dreams came to pass. Joseph was God-gebraically elevated to a position of being second in command over all of Egypt. We see God-gebra at work once more because Joseph was not an Egyptian. Therefore, he should have never been promoted to this position. This position was only reserved for Egyptians with a pedigreed blood line. Also, he had a prison record and you know how hard it is for an ex-convict to receive gainful employment after being released from prison. After the rules of promotion, and the prison record said, "No!" God-gebra still said, "Yes!" God allowed Joseph to have control over all the food in the land. He had authority in Egypt and the entire known world at that time (Gen. 41:37-57). What a mighty God we serve!

As mentioned earlier, the X-treme makeover process is not complete until after revealing yourself to friends and family so they can evaluate its results. The Bible says that because of a famine in the land Joseph's brothers had to come back to Egypt to seek food and provision (Genesis 42:7). Look at God! The very ones that betrayed Joseph and sold him away because of their jealously, are the very ones that God places in His path and because of the favor of God, Joseph is placed in a position (like his dreams foretold) to decide whether they will live or die.

"And Joseph saw his brethren, and he knew them, but made himself strange unto them, and spake roughly unto them; and he said unto them, Whence come ye? And they said, From the land of Canaan to buy food. And Joseph knew his brethren, but they knew not him" (Gen 42:8-9).

After reading this account, there is a question that still remains unanswered, why didn't Joseph's brothers recognize him? After all, they were raised up with him. I imagine prior to selling him into slavery, they dined at the same dinner table with him; they even shared the same living quarters. So what would make it so terribly difficult for them to make a positive identification? Joseph's X-treme Makeover instituted by the favor and anointing of God made him unrecognizable. So much so, that Joseph had to re-introduce himself to his own brothers.

"Joseph said unto his brethren, I am Joseph: doth my father yet live? And his brethren could not answer him; for they were troubled at his presence. And Joseph said to his brethren, Come near to me, I pray you. And they came near. And he said, I am Joseph your brother, whom ye sold into Egypt" (Gen 45:3-4).

Joseph's X-treme Makeover is complete as he reveals to his brothers the alterations and modifications that God has made in his life since they last met. After all it was Joseph that had been stripped of his coat (Gen. 37:23), sold out (Gen. 37:28), tempted (Gen. 39:7), lied on (Gen. 39:14), and ultimately forgotten (Gen 40:23). But he encourages his brothers by telling them, *"be not grieved nor angry with yourselves, that ye sold me hither: for God did send me before you to preserve life* (Gen. 45:5). *But as for you, ye thought evil against me; but God meant it unto good, to bring to pass, as it is this day, to save much people alive"* (Gen. 50:20).

Perhaps there is someone reading this book presently that can identify first hand with what Joseph had to endure. You may have been sold out by loved ones, or perhaps you were given up for adoption, lied on, misunderstood, or just maybe you were abandoned and left to fend for yourself without the love and guidance of compassionate parents. But God has made several promises to you along the way. And like Joseph, it doesn't matter what your life may have been like, those promises are still coming to pass. It's only a matter of time until God pulls back the proverbial curtain to reveal the "new you." After your makeover is complete, you too will have to re-introduce yourself. Why? Because those who knew you before are not going to recognize you because previous (pre-makeover) circumstances once said, "you lack the faith to believe it, the motivation to achieve it, or even the finances to own it." However, the value of X (God's promises) has made you a new creature and behold all things have become new.

The irony of the story of Joseph is that the same gracious Hand of the Lord which during Joseph's humiliation, had kept him from sin, depression, disobedience, and despair; now, preserved him in his exaltation from the clutches of pride, arrogance and revenge. Only God-gebra has the ability to make your comeback greater than your setback!

Chapter 6
Five Reasons God Applies
the God-gebra Formula $(a+b+c=x)$

At this stage in God-gebra 101, you should be well acquainted with the ideology and sophistication of the God-gebra principle. But like any good mathematician knows, to become a superior problem solver, you have to apply this formula to an overwhelming group of circumstances in order to see under what parameters this rule works best.

Upon careful examination of the scriptures, I have determined that there are at least 5 reasons that will prompt God to utilize God-gebra. As affirmed in Chapter 1, God-gebra will cause God to "break the rules" in order to fulfill His will for your life. After all, if "All the Glory" belongs to God, then it's His reputation that's on the line should failure result. And we know with God, failure is never a possibility.

There are five reasons God applies God-gebra in the lives of people today:

1. Because of a **Need**
2. In Response to **Faith**
3. To show (Other's) His **Favor** (on your life)
4. **Obedience** to His Word
5. For Our **Salvation**

The very first reason God will make use of God-gebra is…

1. Because of a Need

"Abraham's Need"

> *"And it came to pass after these things, that God did tempt Abraham, and said unto him, Abraham: and he said, Behold, here I am. And he said, Take now thy son, thine only son Isaac, whom thou lovest, and get thee into the land of Moriah; and offer him there for a burnt offering upon one of the mountains which I will tell thee of. And Abraham rose up early in the morning, and saddled his ass, and took two of his young men with him, and Isaac his son, and clave the wood for the burnt offering, and rose up, and went unto the place of which God had told him. Then on the third day Abraham lifted up his eyes, and saw the place afar off. And Abraham said unto his young men, Abide ye here with the ass; and I and the lad will go yonder and worship, and come again to you. And Abraham took the wood of the burnt offering, and laid*

it upon Isaac his son; and he took the fire in his hand, and a knife; and they went both of them together. And Isaac spake unto Abraham his father, and said, My father: and he said, Here am I, my son. And he said, Behold the fire and the wood: but where is the lamb for a burnt offering? And Abraham said, My son, God will provide himself a lamb for a burnt offering: so they went both of them together. And they came to the place which God had told him of; and Abraham built an altar there, and laid the wood in order, and bound Isaac his son, and laid him on the altar upon the wood. And Abraham stretched forth his hand, and took the knife to slay his son. And the angel of the LORD called unto him out of heaven, and said, Abraham, Abraham: and he said, Here am I. And he said, Lay not thine hand upon the lad, neither do thou any thing unto him: for now I know that thou fearest God, seeing thou hast not withheld thy son, thine only son from me. And Abraham lifted up his eyes, and looked, and behold behind him a ram caught in a thicket by his horns: and Abraham went and took the ram, and offered him up for a burnt offering in the stead of his son. And Abraham called the name of that place Jehovahjireh: as it is said to this day, In the mount of the LORD it shall be seen (Gen. 22:1- 14).

In this narrative, Abraham is asked by God to sacrifice his only son. Abraham finds himself in a very difficult position. He doesn't want to kill the only son that he waited until he was nearly 100 years old to have and he doesn't want to disappoint the God that said he would make him the father of many nations. Abraham, like many of us, has a need to be delivered.

As Christians we are not immune from the atrocities found in this world. However, in the midst of trusting God, He will always direct us to a safe haven where His Hand of provision and stability resides.

After God is convinced that Abraham's love for Him supersedes his love for Isaac displayed by his willingness to sacrifice him, God sends an angel to thwart his further attempt to kill his beloved son. Abraham has a need. Do you have any needs that warrant God's attention?

Upon further examination of these scriptures, it seems ridiculous that God would ask Abraham to kill the son He promised to him in the first place. Why? Because conventional wisdom asks, "Why would God perform the miracle of fertilizing Sarah's lifeless womb only to allow their son (Isaac) to die at the hand of the father to which he was promised?" This is where God-gebra intervenes.

Godgebra Applied…Situation Solved

Notice what God does. He responds to the need of Abraham by directing his attention to a ram that just so happens to be caught in the thicket at the precise time of Abraham's need.

"And Abraham lifted up his eyes, and looked, and behold behind him a ram caught in a thicket by his horns" (Gen. 22:13).

Think about it. The scripture indicates that the ram was caught by the horns. I personally believe it was placed there intentionally, without the possibility of escape. It baffles and befuddles my mind to consider that the majestic Hand of God planted the ram in the thicket long before Abraham ever had a need, because He foreknew there would be a necessity, to which He predestined a way of escape, in order to resolve Abraham's impending dilemma. Wow! God is awesome! He declares the ending of a situation from the beginning (Isa. 46:10).

When God's people suffer, He is attentive to our every need. He is a doting Father that comes to the rescue after hearing the desperate cries of His children and He will use all means at His disposal to respond to each and every one of our needs.

My mind goes back to a testimony service I attended one night at my former church. During this service, I remember hearing the tear jerking account of a single mother with three children struggling to make ends meet. This faithful mother needed transportation desperately as she and her three children were riding the city bus back and forth to church. The mother went on to explain how she went from dealership to dealership looking for a car but unfortunately, she kept getting declined because of a poor credit history resulting from a loss of employment. She said this one particular day during prayer, God spoke to her and said, "I am going to meet your needs, if you trust me." She began to tear up as she gasped for breath in between her verbal pauses. She said she proceeded to go into a dealership that she had never visited in hopes that they might finally approve her but before she could get to the door, she heard a voice say, "Go back to the dealership where you were declined." You could sense the hesitancy in her voice as she described her feelings of rejection resulting from being denied initially by this same dealership. Nevertheless, at the Word of the Lord, she arrived at this dealership and that "still soft voice" returned and said, "Go to the same salesman that declined you originally." She said she walked over to the salesman who recognized her instantly and said, "I am here to pick up my new car." The salesmen laughed facetiously and replied, "Come over to my desk and have a seat." She explained that the salesman pulled out her file to reveal the previous documentation which verified that she had been previously declined. The salesman out of respect asked, if her job situation had changed? She said, "No." By this time another gentleman walks up and joins the conversation by asking, "Didn't I see you in here before?" She responded, "Yes." The mother went on to say that the man acted as if he knew her and wanted to know why she didn't purchase a car during her first visit to the dealership. She told him she did not have any money and unfortunately, her credit was tarnished, but God said come back to this dealership as He was going to supply my need for transportation. She said the minute she told him God sent her, he confessed that there was something different about her when she walked through the doors. He said he felt as if his mission was to somehow get her into the car of her choice and not the advertised monthly special (Look at God!). By this time, the mother is trying to hold her composure as she jumps up and down shaking the keys to a brand new Cadillac. It turns out that the mysterious man was the owner of the Cadillac Dealership and he subsequently told her to pick out the car she wanted.

She ended her testimony as the church went into a radical praise by encouraging the people of God. She shouted, "I didn't have any money, my credit was bad, but God spoke into my spirit that He was going to meet my need according to His Riches in Glory."

God-gebra had broken the rules for this woman because she walked into the dealership with no political clout, without a celebrity name, but she drove off in a "Brand New" Cadillac of her choosing with "Praises on Her Lips". Hallelujah! I still get stirred up when I think about how God is a Need-Meeter!

Be encouraged and remember if God knows that you have a critical need, He will exceedingly meet your needs even if it means breaking the rules to do it. After all, he is JehovahJireh our provider.

The second reason God applies God-gebra is in direct response to our faith.

2. Response to Faith

"The Canaanite Woman's Faith"

> *"Then Jesus went thence, and departed into the coasts of Tyre and Sidon. And, behold, a woman of Canaan came out of the same coasts, and cried unto him, saying, Have mercy on me, O Lord, thou Son of David; my daughter is grievously vexed with*

a devil. But he answered her not a word. And his disciples came and besought him, saying, Send her away; for she crieth after us. But he answered and said, I am not sent but unto the lost sheep of the house of Israel. Then came she and worshipped him, saying, Lord, help me. But he answered and said, It is not meet to take the children's bread, and to cast it to dogs. And she said, Truth, Lord: yet the dogs eat of the crumbs which fall from their masters' table. Then Jesus answered and said unto her, O woman, great is thy faith: be it unto thee even as thou wilt. And her daughter was made whole from that very hour" (Mark 7:24-30).

This storyline illustrates the potency power of Faith and its ability to incite God to apply God-gebra like an adhesive, in order to bond your need to the much anticipated blessing.

As we read above, this woman came to Jesus with a very needy request. Her request was not a selfish one, it was not even for her but for her daughter's sake as the girl was demon possessed. The pain, anguish and hope in the mother's voice could be compared to any mother pleading for the life and well being of her child. Yet she was met with enough discouragement to move her and many of us for that matter, to the point of giving up.

Jesus allowed the Canaanite woman to be attacked with discouragement at least four times on the day she needed His help the most.

1. The first attack—Jesus ignores her.
2. The second attack—The disciples yell, send her away.
3. The third attack—Jesus says He has nothing to do with her as she is not part of his lineage (Jewish).
4. The fourth attack—He insults and degrades her by calling her a dog.

Think about it. How successful would a Christian ministry be, if the pastor totally ignored you? For the sake of discussion, let's say you walked into the pastor's office with a heavy burden on your shoulders, and no matter how many times you asked him for help and benevolence, he gave you yet another reason to just give up in frustration and walk away. What would you do? This is what the world would have expected the Canaanite woman to do. Just walk away!

God-gebra Applied…Situation Solved

What do you suppose could have been running through this mother's mind after receiving such a hearty rebuke? Could she have begun entertaining the possibility that Jesus did not want to help her? I believe that's a possibility. The silence of Jesus here in the pages of Matthew has been magnified one thousand fold in the minds and hearts of hurting and rejected Christians everywhere. When answers do not come when we expect them, it is easy enough to just lose faith and give up. Yet this Canaanite woman did not give up! This is the point where God-gebra is carefully applied.

Look again at how the Canaanite woman reacted to this barrage of discouraging and degrading words. When Jesus ignored her, and called her a dog, she could have rolled her eyes and put her hands on her hips and said something like, "You have gone too far with your insults, aren't you (Jesus)—supposed to be a man of love and mercy, and yet you treat me, a humble women who has a legitimate need, with such disrespect.... I'm leaving here, I didn't ask for this! But, instead of acting that way, she remained humbled and persistent in prayer by saying, *"Truth Lord, but even the dogs feed on the crumbs which fall from the masters table."* In other words, she was willing and ready to receive whatever crumbs Jesus tossed her way, because even those crumbs would be "more than enough" to fulfill her prayerful request.

She was able to press pass the insults, and break through the discouraging words that came her way because of one simple truth. She trusted and believed in all the things that she heard about Jesus. This faith-filled woman knew Him to be the Messiah, because she called Him "the Son of David." She believed that Jesus had the power to heal her daughter of the demon possession. Because of this belief, she rested her hopes on all that she heard about Jesus. Jesus in turn saw her unwavering faith, bull dog tenacity, and the fact that she wasn't leaving without her blessing. This compelled Jesus to eventually say, "Woman, your faith is great, it shall be done for you as you wish."

The irony of this story is that traditional laws actually prohibited Jesus from having any contact with this woman (let alone healing her) because she was a Canaanite woman. But God-gebra was applied because her faith simply could not be ignored. Jesus (God manifest in the flesh) is attracted to faith the same way magnets are attracted to metal. Faith is a type of aphrodisiac to God, and if He becomes stimulated and aroused by seeing your faith on display, He will bypass political affiliation, social reformation and even racial domination to give you too, the desires of your heart, even if the rules say otherwise. He is just that kind of God!

The third reason God applies God-gebra is to show "His Favor" on your life.

3. To Show (Others) His Favor
"David Anointed King"

> *"And it came to pass, when they were come, that he looked on Eli'ab, and said, Surely the LORD's anointed is before him. But the LORD said unto Samuel, Look not on his countenance, or on the height of his stature; because I have refused him: for the LORD seeth not as man seeth; for man looketh on the outward appearance, but the LORD looketh on the heart. Then Jesse called Abin'adab, and made him pass before Samuel. And he said, Neither hath the LORD chosen this. Then Jesse made Shammah to pass by. And he said, Neither hath the LORD chosen this. Again, Jesse made seven of his sons to pass before Samuel. And Samuel said unto Jesse, The LORD hath not chosen these. And Samuel said unto Jesse, Are here all thy children? And he said, There remaineth*

yet the youngest, and, behold, he keepeth the sheep. And Samuel said unto Jesse, Send and fetch him: for we will not sit down till he come hither. And he sent, and brought him in. Now he was ruddy, and withal of a beautiful countenance, and goodly to look to. And the LORD said, Arise, anoint him: for this is he" (1 Sam. 16:6-12).

To briefly summarize, Samuel the prophet was instructed by God to visit Jesse's (David's father) house and while there, he was to find and anoint the next King of Israel. Upon arriving, Jesse began to parade his seven sons before Samuel. At first glance, they possessed all the external characteristics; age, stature, seniority, experience and their father's favor that would cause Samuel to assume one of them would be the next King of Israel. But ironically, you can have man's favor but not God's. When you possess God's favor, He will give you favor with man (Prov.16:7)—not the other way around. God warns Samuel not to base his decision on what he sees because characteristics that are pleasing to man are rejected by God (1 Sam.16:7). God has X-ray vision and sees beyond the many facades we erect in order to conceal our true identity and motives. Sure enough, God says, "I have rejected all seven of these scrapping, dashing young men." As his options are narrowing, Samuel asks, "Jesse is there another son perhaps that I have missed?" Jesse pauses a moment as if to say, "I have one more son, but surely it couldn't be him that God has chosen to anoint King of Israel." Jesse further replies, "He is the youngest and is currently out back with the sheep." In other words, David's own father rejects and forsakes his ability. This is the point where God takes out His spiritual chalkboard and starts applying God-gebra in order to show forth His favor after everyone has rejected and thrown in the towel on David.

God-gebra Applied...Situation Solved

Sound familiar to anyone? You may be in a situation currently that is similar to David's where the odds are against you. Get ready to receive the victory! God has an uncanny ability to place his anointing and favor on individuals that are considered by others to be unworthy and undeserving. As a matter of fact, if this were a high school mock election, God would deliberately pick the person labeled most unlikely to succeed and anoint them which now qualifies them to be most likely to succeed. The more unworthy you are considered by others is reversed to reveal how valuable you are in God's eyes. God is dyslexic, which means He operates backwards in order to move His plan forward. He created the end first and then backed up to allow eternity to intersect with time. At this point of intersection, God-gebra is revealed.

And if we could ask David, I am sure he would attest that if you've been rejected, passed over or just plain forgotten but God's favor is on your life, He will indeed make the last, first (Matt. 19:30). I can imagine when David was crowned King of Israel, during his inauguration, he probably took the podium, and in front of all those who previously questioned his qualifications, he declared humbly but without reservation, "God-gebra, like Favor, Just Isn't Fair! Hallelujah!

The fourth reason God applies God-gebra is because of your Obedience to His Word.

4. Obedience

"Behold, to obey is better than sacrifice, and to hearken than the fat of rams" (1 Sam. 15:22).

What does it really mean to be obedient to God's Word? It represents far more than just methodically performing a set of duties in a ritualistic fashion. Obedience is not only subjection to an external law, *but it requires the surrendering of my will to the authority of another.* Therefore, obedience to God is the heart's recognition of His supreme deity: of His right to rule and command, and our duty to honor and comply regardless of the request. Obedience is the complete subjection of our will to the covenant of Jesus Christ.

"Godliness is profitable unto all things" (I Tim. 4:8). By obedience we purify our souls (I Pet. 1:21). By obedience, we obtain the ear of God (I John 3:22), just as disobedience is an obstruction to our prayers (Jer. 5:25; Isa. 59:2). By practicing obedience, we show forth our love to God and in turn, He intimately manifests Himself unto us (John 14:21). As we journey this Christian walk, we learn that if we completely submit to God, we will experience joyousness and a level of peace that passes all understanding. Because of obedience to God's Word, we learn that "His commandments are *not* grievous" (I John 5:3), and most importantly, "in keeping of them there is great reward" (Psa. 19:11).

I find that most Christians tend to be obedient to God's Word so long as the request is not "unrealistic" and still coincides with their ability to see the result of their obedient actions. However, the problem lies when God instructs us to perform tasks that appear uncharacteristic, unorthodox or perhaps they are repetitive (we tried it that way before). At this point our obedience is challenged because in our minds, we can't see how the execution of an "unseemly task" will result in our being delivered or receiving the victory. Let's review a case study involving obedience and its influence on the power of God-gebra.

"The Big Catch"

> *"And it came to pass, that, as the people pressed upon him to hear the word of God, he stood by the lake of Gennesaret, And saw two ships standing by the lake: but the fishermen were gone out of them, and were washing their nets. And he entered into one of the ships, which was Simon's, and prayed him that he would thrust out a little from the land. And he sat down, and taught the people out of the ship. Now when he had left speaking, he said unto Simon, Launch out into the deep, and*

let down your nets for a draught. And Simon answering said
unto him, Master, we have toiled all the night, and have taken
nothing: nevertheless at thy word I will let down the net. And
when they had this done, they inclosed a great multitude of
fishes: and their net brake" (Luke 5:1-6).

A brief synopsis of this story reveals that Simon has fished all
night, having caught nothing and is completing the arduous task
of cleaning his nets. Out of nowhere, Jesus gets on his boat and
tells him to launch out a bit from the shore. Jesus then instructs
Simon to "let down his nets." Now remember our discussion
point a couple of paragraphs ago (regarding obedience) in which
we determined, the problem with obedience lies when God
instructs us to perform tasks that appear uncharacteristic,
unorthodox or perhaps they are repetitive (we tried it that way
before). Simon had been there and done that! He was a fisherman.
He knew the cyclical feeding habits of fish. Yet Jesus challenges
Simon's obedience based upon his past failures.

God-gebra Applied…Situation Solved

How many of you have tried something and it failed? Maybe
you attempted to start a business, write a book, buy a house, go
back to school or even start a ministry and it failed miserably. This
is the point where God applies God-gebra. He takes a piece of
spiritual white chalk and begins to blot out your past failures
because of your obedience to His Word.

As our story resumes, Simon says something that rejuvenates and resurrects his lifeless situation. He responds to Jesus request by saying, *"nevertheless"*, which can be interpreted, "I don't see it or necessarily believe it, but because you said it Lord, I will honor your request."

This is the level of obedience that God wants us to maintain. He wants to show us miracles but in order for us to see these awesome manifestations of His Word, we have to be obedient. I don't care how ridiculous the request. To coin a phrase from Nike, "JUST DO IT!"

I want to draw your attention to a very important theological principle regarding this text. Notice, Simon still has a little trepidation regarding Jesus' request. How do I know? Look at Simon's actions. Jesus tells him to let down his nets (plural) and Simon (the Bible notes), only let's down one net. Many of us want to "safeguard" God's request by not honoring it completely—as if to say, in the event of failure, I can still salvage what little I have left instead of losing everything. But regardless of our finite interpretation of God's intentions, the command said, "Let down your nets! Not let down your net."

As the story concludes, God-gebra is activated by the Word of Jesus and Simon ultimately receives the blessing—"A Net Breaking Blessing." He catches so many fish that his net cannot accommodate the over abundance and begins to break. Let's state for the record, that acting in obedience to God's seemingly redundant request yielded a bountiful harvest after all, whereas, man's conventional wisdom was proven once more to be inadequate. Similarly, if we learn to be obedient to God's Word, we too will see the miraculous and unfathomable wonders of God-gebra in our lives.

Speaking of unfathomable works of God, my wife recently reminded me of a testimony that we both heard regarding obedience and the miracles it will provoke. On Thanksgiving Day at my former church there would be an annual worship service held called, "A Graceful Thanksgiving." During these services a few Saints of God would share actual "thankfulness" testimonies with the congregation at large. Well, this one particular testimony was so awesome that I felt compelled to encourage you (the reader) with its contents.

The "Power" of Obedience

There was a lady at the church who began to testify before the people of God. She quickly started to tear up as she grabbed the microphone to share her testimony. She began by saying, a couple of weeks ago there was a bad snow storm that caused tremendous electrical damage in her neighborhood and as a result of this damage, there were several power lines down leaving her subsequently without power. She couldn't even make a phone call to report the damage to Detroit Edison (Electrical Company) because the phone didn't work. She went on to say that she was a single parent raising her children. She said her son suffers from a medical condition that causes him to experience life threatening convulsions and seizures. Well, during this snow storm, she was awakened in the middle of the night to the sound of her son's hysterical screams and his gasps for air as he couldn't breathe. She noticed that her son's complexion was fading as he was having a seizure. She said her son had experienced seizures in the past but when she heard the pitch and tone of his screeches, she realized that this was the worst one to date. Her son was hollering loudly as his eyes began to roll back to reveal the whites of his eyes and with each gasp for breath, it became more difficult for him to attempt the next one. She said she realized by his excruciating and tormenting screams of agony, that if she didn't get him immediate medical attention, he could possibly die. Instinctively, she picks up the telephone and dials Emergency 911. She said there was a man's voice on the other line that answered and said, "Operator, how can I help you?" She said frantically, "My son is having a seizure and is having trouble breathing and I don't know how long he can hang on. His complexion is already turning a faint blue." The operator said he would dispatch someone to her home immediately. So she hung up the phone and began to pray for her son. She said she remembered petitioning God by saying, "Lord I want to be obedient to your Word because only your Word can save my son." As she prayed, she heard a voice tell her that because she honored God through her obedience to His Word, everything was going to be all right. By this point, the entire church was on the verge of erupting like a volcano. The church was silent. Everyone (including myself) was hanging on her every word. She went on to say, suddenly, there was a knock at the door and a voice said, "EMS, open up!" She hurried and opened the door and the EMS rushed her son to the hospital like a scene on the television show ER. After arriving at the hospital, the doctors notified her that her son would have to remain overnight for subsequent testing but he would make a full recovery. (Hallelujah!)

She concluded her testimony to reveal the most extraordinary crescendo I had ever heard. She said the next day, a Detroit Edison technician appeared at her door and told her that he was there to repair the down wires and restore power to her phone lines. In utter amazement, she asked the repairman, were the phone lines down last night? He emphatically said, "Yes! As a matter of fact, they have been down for the last 48 hours." She immediately ran to her phone and picked it up to verify that her phone was in fact dead. And guess what, her phone was still dead "as a door knob". At that point the entire church went into a frenzied praise shouting…Hallelujah!!! May God be praised!

That leaves us with a couple of unanswered questions. If the phone was dead for 48 hours as verified by the repairman, who answered the telephone? Where did the operator come from? Whose voice was on the other end? How did the call get through to Emergency dispatch without Power! We may never really know the answer to these questions. Perhaps her prayers dialed the heavenly host and Gabriel, God's chief messenger, answered and sent help. Or maybe because of her unwavering faith, she was granted spiritual wireless capability. No matter what you choose to believe, one thing for sure, her son is still alive and she credited her obedience to God's Word for her miracle—and because of the proven effectiveness of God-gebra, I am certainly inclined to believe her.

Our God Is an Awesome God!

The last reason that God applies God-gebra is to bring Salvation to the world.

5. For "Our" Salvation

"And Joshua the son of Nun sent out of Shittim two men to spy secretly, saying, Go view the land, even Jericho. And they went, and came into an harlot's house, named Rahab, and lodged there" (Josh. 2:1).

In chapter 4 we discussed the "Hall of Faith" and determined that Rahab (the harlot) was named along with the "who's who" list of notables in the Bible. She was inducted into the "Hall of Faith" because she hid the spies that Joshua sent into the land (Jericho). She risked her life and the life of her family to save God's chosen people.

"By faith the harlot Rahab perished not with them that believed not, when she had received the spies with peace" (Heb. 11:31).

One of the most amazing things to me in all scripture is…
"How could Rahab the harlot be in the lineage of Jesus?" (Matt.
1:5). Rahab and Ruth were the only non-Jews in the lineage of
Jesus, but Rahab was the only harlot! How could the pure, long-
awaited, holy Messiah come through a harlot's lineage? God's
ways (God-gebra) are truly mysterious!

In Joshua 2:1 we have the first mention of Rahab being a
harlot in the Bible. In fact the Bible uses this language of Rahab
being a harlot five times. Even though thousands of years have
passed since she lived and all her good works of faith were done,
she is still identified and labeled not by her faith but by her
vocation (a harlot) in many church sermons across this nation.
Why is that? I was under the impression that once our sins are
forgiven they are then thrown into the sea of forgetfulness.
Perhaps there is a greater message to be understood about whom
she was and why God chose her out of all people, to fulfill His
purpose. I believe Rahab has a message for all of us and God has
placed it in the scriptures for our maturation and instruction.
"Now all these things happened unto them for examples: and they are written
for our admonition, upon whom the ends of the world are come" (1 Cor.
10:11).

I know many of you are probably thinking, "How could a
harlot's life be beneficial for my instruction?" Certainly the faith
she exhibited demonstrates the potential we all have; yet she also
reminds and teaches us to not judge. Still, how many of us would
expect a great act of faith to have come from a hooker? As quiet
as it's kept, many of us would not only have walked by her house,

but crossed to the other side of the street so as not to be contaminated by her sinful deeds. Unfortunately, from what we know of prostitution, realities then and now, we envision a woman that is not dressed in "Sunday best", but for a "Saturday night special". Only by facing the reality of Rahab's life, can we truly learn from her. Think about it, her society would have rejected her because her career daily exposed her to dirty, possibly diseased men who sought to use her for one purpose only. But God still allows her to be a chalkboard for the likes of God-gebra to teach us a valuable lesson. I believe God placed her as an example to us because after all is said and done; God-gebra changed her life!

The way we typically view Rahab in the flesh is as a harlot. The Bible conveys,

> *"For to be carnally minded is death; but to be spiritually minded is life and peace. Because the carnal mind is enmity against God: for it is not subject to the law of God, neither indeed can be. So then they that are in the flesh cannot please God"* (Rom. 8:6-8).

When our minds are rooted in the flesh we display hostility or enmity towards God. This is why Paul instructed us to be transformed by the renewing of our minds (Rom.12:2). In order to please the heart of God, we have to resist sin, which casts out "Stinking Thinking". Don't be fooled. The mind and body individually do not represent evil, but the mind when focused on the ways of the flesh is, because it provokes the body to commit evil deeds. Our mind has been diabolically programmed to sin against God since the fall of man in the garden. But now, Jesus has come through the power of Calvary's cross to re-program and redeem us from the eternal curse of sin and death. Humanity since the fall of man has been plagued by three kinds of sins:

1. Lust of the Eye
2. Lust of the Flesh
3. Pride of Life

> *"For all that is in the world, the lust of the flesh, and the lust of the eyes, and the pride of life, is not of the Father, but is of the world"* (1 John 2:16).

Each of these worldly attributes in our life can be overcome by the Salvation of Jesus Christ. As a result, Rahab becomes an ideal candidate for God to illustrate His life changing love for the socially disenfranchised that are typically snubbed and labeled as being "unsavable." God purposely selects these types of individuals to show us the unrestricted, non biased cleansing power of salvation that we "all" need.

God-gebra applied…Situation Solved

> *"And Salmon begat Booz of Rachab; and Booz begat Obed of Ruth; and Obed begat Jesse; And Jesse begat David the*

king; and David the king begat Solomon of her that had been the wife of Urias; And Solomon begat Roboam; and Roboam begat Abia; and Abia begat Asa; And Asa begat Josaphat; and Josaphat begat Joram; and Joram begat Ozias;And Ozias begat Joatham; and Joatham begat Achaz; and Achaz begat Ezekias; And Ezekias begat Manasses; and Manasses begat Amon; and Amon begat Josias; And Josias begat Jechonias and his brethren, about the time they were carried away to Babylon: And after they were brought to Babylon, Jechonias begat Salathiel;and Salathiel begat Zorobabel; And Zorobabel begat Abiud; and Abiud begat Eliakim; and Eliakim begat Azor; And Azor begat Sadoc; and Sadoc begat Achim; and Achim begat Eliud; And Eliud begat Eleazar; and Eleazar begat Matthan; and Matthan begat Jacob; And Jacob begat Joseph the husband of Mary, of whom was born Jesus, who is called Christ" (Matt. 1:1-16).

The fact that Rahab was in the lineage of Jesus speaks prophetic utterings to us that our minds and hearts *can* be changed once we have an encounter with God, despite our previous background.

Rahab is a poster-child for God-gebra as she represents hurting and rejected people all over this world who are not supposed to be used of God because of past or present discretions. Rahab was a prostitute and for all intensive purposes she was the epitome of "needing justification."

Maybe you come from the other side of the tracks or grew up participating in activities spawned by your environment where all you saw as part of a normal day's events were pimps, pushers; prostitution, family abuse, carjacking and other instances of societal decay. Whatever your situation, God-gebra will erase your emotional scars and numb your physical pains in order to bring you to the point of salvation (Acts 2:38).

If it were possible to go online and look up a picture of Jesus' family tree, who would have ever believed you would see Rahab the prostitute, with her red mini skirt, fish net stockings and high heeled stilettos smiling along side some of the greatest men and women in the Bible. After God applied God-gebra to her life, instead of walking down "Rodeo Drive" in search of a date, she is now seated in "Heavenly Places" with Christ Jesus. She may not be celebrated on Hollywood Boulevard's "walk of fame," but now she will be associated throughout eternity with Jesus' name. That's what true salvation is all about. Allowing the love displayed on Calvary's Cross by the shed blood of Jesus Christ to be the "complimentary" admission ticket that grants "everyone" equal access to enter into eternity. God is an Equal Opportunity Redeemer!

Only God-gebra can break the rules and allow an unworthy prostitute access into the royal family by adding her to the genealogy of Jesus Christ.

One final summary reveals that God applies God-gebra because of 5 reasons: A Need, Faith, Favor, Obedience and Salvation. If you find yourself currently in a situation that looks like there is no way out and you have at least one of these five characteristics, God-gebra is primed and ready to work a miracle just for you!

"X" Marks the Spot...
Final Thoughts

On an authentic treasure map the most valuable point is identified by an "X". As a point of reference, an exploration is not considered a success until after you have physically found the location of "X". At the point when the longitude and latitude coordinates finally reveal the positioning of X; there is a sense of exhilaration and excitement. Enthusiasm builds because there is a belief that something "priceless" is about to be uncovered for the first time. This literary journey has been similar to that of searching for a valuable treasure. Why? You might be wondering. The Bible states, *"Again, the kingdom of heaven is like unto treasure hid in a field; the which when a man hath found, he hideth, and for joy thereof goeth and selleth all that he hath, and buyeth that field"* (Matt. 13:44).

The Bible likens the Kingdom of God to searching for the elusive "X" which identifies the exact point of the corresponding treasure. However, the X that the scripture notes is a bit different. Let me explain.

> *"Therefore if any man be in Christ, he is a new creature: old things are passed away; behold, all things are become new"* (2 Cor. 5:17).

Throughout this manuscript, God-gebra acted as a literary tour guide while we journeyed in search of The Value of "X". According to the Book of 2 Corinthians, when Jesus Christ sanctifies and cleanses us, every sin committed before fulfilling the requirements of salvation has been negated, canceled, or crossed out. So by definition, X signifies the Cross of Calvary. Ironically if you were to hold up the letter X at an angle, it would look identical to a cross. Our salvation process began at Calvary when The Value of X (God) hung on the cross as a reproach for our sins.

At Calvary, Jesus (God manifest in the flesh) nailed lust and X-tasy, XXX-citement, X-tra marital affairs, and all other dastardly sins to the cross. And as a result, God-gebra (God's Miraculous Works) emancipated us by making us X-fornicators, X-liars, X-cheaters and X-sinners because as we stated earlier, *If any man be in Christ he is a new creature because he has received the power of (X) and Old things have past away behold all things became new.*

God's rationale for performing the impossible, confounding the wise, raising the dead, giving sight to the blind, healing the sick, unstopping deaf ears, cleansing lepers, casting out devils, turning water to wine, stilling the storms and ultimately saving mankind from a fiery grave called hell is what God-gebra exists to fulfill.

God's love and compassion towards humanity is evidenced by His ability to show forth His undeniable power at Calvary's Cross in order to convince us to faithfully believe that there are... No Impossibilities, Only Realities with God-gebra!

Final Thoughts...

In the halls of academia, whenever a class nears the end of a semester, students tend to reflect upon the courses learning to determine how best, if at all, to apply the newly acquired knowledge with the goal of impacting and enhancing their lives and communities moving forward.

As God-gebra101, The Value of X comes to a close, my prayer is that you (the reader) will reflect upon the many revelations, disappointments, testimonies and triumphs that God has given throughout this manuscript and begin applying these invaluable learning's to your lives as you strive to walk "In Spirit and in Truth."

Don't keep this blessing a secret! Encourage someone else so that God-gebra might work in their lives as they Discover...The Value of "X".

-To God Be the Glory-

IRB